SUPERHERO LEADERSHIP

SUPERHERO LEADERSHIP

28 Ways to Lead with Courage, Strength, and Compassion

PETER CUNEO

**Former CEO of MARVEL Entertainment
with Joe Garner**

∧
PEAKPOINT
— PRESS —

All rights reserved. No part of this book may be reproduced in any manner without the express written consent of the publisher, except in the case of brief excerpts in critical reviews or articles. All inquiries should be addressed to Skyhorse Publishing, 307 West 36th Street, 11th Floor, New York, NY 10018.

Peakpoint Press books may be purchased in bulk at special discounts for sales promotion, corporate gifts, fund-raising, or educational purposes. Special editions can also be created to specifications. For details, contact the Special Sales Department, Skyhorse Publishing, 307 West 36th Street, 11th Floor, New York, NY 10018 or info@skyhorsepublishing.com.

Peakpoint® and Peakpoint Press® are registered trademarks of Skyhorse Publishing, Inc.®, a Delaware corporation.

Visit our website at www.skyhorsepublishing.com.

10 9 8 7 6 5 4 3 2 1

Library of Congress Cataloging-in-Publication Data is available on file.

Jacket design by David Ter-Avanesyan
Cover Artwork by Sergio Cariello, Brett R. Smith & Eric Weathers

ISBN: 978-1-5107-8384-3

Ebook ISBN: 978-1-5107-8385-0

Printed in the United States of America

Many years ago, I got lucky and met the love of my life, my wife, Maris. Through thick and thin, she was always there to support my adventures. She gifted me with two great sons and amazing grandkids. Without her there was no me. She is as much a part of this book as I am.

Heroes are made by the path they choose, not the powers they are graced with.

—Tony Stark, *Iron Man*

TABLE OF CONTENTS

YOU DON'T KNOW HOW GOOD YOU ARE

Facing a crisis situation is part of leadership. What do you do when things go south? Like an airline pilot, things may be routine most of the time, but you really earn your money when events are *anything but normal.*

I've built a career as a turnaround CEO, moving from crisis to crisis. My career became a little like the plot of a Marvel superhero movie . . . there aren't many routine days for Captain America or Iron Man.

Marvel is one of my most notable turnaround situations, so it was fitting to theme this book around being a superhero in the business world.

But before we get to the lessons I've learned about leadership, particularly in the challenge of turnarounds, let me share the story of my own travels and what lead to my risk-oriented personality.

The Adventurer Gene

People often asked how I learned leadership, and why I've chosen what many see as the riskier path in life and business. People assume I must've been trained that way, maybe in business school or during turnarounds where I was a junior participant. But the truth is, that spirit didn't come from a classroom or a boardroom. It's been part of me for as long as I can remember.

Simply, I was born with the "adventurer gene."

Of course, there's no actual genetic science behind that. But I am a descendant of parents and grandparents who lived boldly, who saw the world not as something to fear, but something to explore. The mindset of pushing boundaries and trusting your abilities even when the odds looked stacked was passed down to me through stories and the way they lived their lives.

Let's start with my grandparents.

Peter and Christine MacLeod immigrated to the US from Nova Scotia, their ancestors originally from the Isle of Skye, in the Scottish Highlands. My grandfather, Peter MacLeod, a lion of a man and the namesake of my middle name, worked steamships around the world. He once mined for gold in Rhodesia, where his brother was tragically killed.

They came to America in the early 1920s, settling in Manhattan. Peter became Grand Commander of the New York State Masons, despite never having more than a high school education. Christine became a nurse.

On the other side of my family, my grandparents were just as colorful and bold.

My grandfather, Frank, was first-generation Italian, that's where the name *Cuneo* comes from. And my grandmother, Betty, came from Sweden, the youngest of ten children. She immigrated to America on her own when she was just twenty years old.

The way my grandparents, Frank and Betty, met feels like something straight out of *Downton Abbey*. They were what you'd call "downstairs" people, working in a luxury apartment building owned by Vincent Astor on the Upper East Side in New York City. My grandmother operated the elevator back when elevators were manual and required an attendant. My grandfather was the building's handyman. Their paths crossed, quite literally, in that elevator. That's where it all began.

They attended Madison Avenue Presbyterian Church, where their children, my parents, Frank and Marion, would eventually meet and, in 1942, marry in that very same church.

My father, Frank, had just joined the navy as an air cadet. He had been a three-year all-city athlete at Stuyvesant High and played basketball at the University of North Carolina. He went on to serve as a navy officer and air navigator in World War II.

He'd been discharged after the war, but with the outbreak of the Korean War, he was called him back into service. Our family moved from New York to military bases across the country, first to Jacksonville, Florida; Bremerton, Washington; San Diego, California, before finally settling in Philadelphia, Pennsylvania, where his tour of duty concluded.

This movement to four cities in two years was the start of my exposure to diversity in people. Four moves. Four sets of friends.

Back in New York, he rejoined the fire department and worked his way up to lieutenant. He was stationed in Chinatown, where fires were especially difficult to battle. Most buildings were old five- and six-story lofts, packed tight and tough to navigate.

My First Lessons in Leadership

When I was thirteen, I saw firsthand how his men respected him, not for his rank, but because he went inside with them, into the flames. That shaped my earliest ideas of leadership: not about titles, but presence, courage, and sharing the risk of jumping into the fire.

Later, after my own navy service in Vietnam, I saw the weight he carried. His survivor's guilt from World War II never left him. Retirement brought frustration. His drinking became a way to numb the pain, sometimes erupting in violence. As a teen, I had to restrain him. Reconciling the father who had taught and protected me with the man he became took decades, but it shaped my understanding of strength, loyalty, and forgiveness.

My mother's spirit shaped me just as much. Like my father, she was a natural athlete, with the kind of swimming and diving talent that might well have taken her to the Olympics. She spent over thirty years working in emergency rooms—as an ER assistant, emergency medical technician (EMT), and later as an EMT dispatcher. When I was a teenager, back when there were no strict regulations regarding ride-a-longs in ambulances, she'd let me accompany her to calls. I watched her stay calm in the worst situations, and it left a lasting mark on me.

One night, a man was decapitated in a car accident on the then new Long Island Expressway in Queens; she walked through the chaos, holding his head, focused and steady. That image seared into me: leadership is about showing up, staying calm under pressure, doing the hard thing without flinching.

What the Big Apple Taught Me

The lessons I learned from both my parents shaped how I understood leadership—not the kind that comes from titles or badges, but the kind that's earned by being there when it matters most. My parents and my grandparents needed to be "out there" and were not happy sitting at a desk.

I grew up in the melting pot of New York City, specifically Queens, one of the most diverse places in the country. I went to school with kids from every background imaginable. Different races, religions, cultures, you name it. And the thing was, we all got along. I never really thought about ethnic differences. We just learned together, played together. It felt normal.

Looking back, though, I was quietly learning how to navigate different personalities and points of view. I didn't think of it as leadership training, but in a way, that's exactly what it was.

In high school, I stayed involved in things I loved, like mixed chorus, even though I had no singing talent. I remember having to audition with a solo, which terrified me. I knew I didn't have the greatest voice, but somehow the chorus director let me in. He was a real leader. He took this diverse group of kids and made us sound great. Nobody quit. He created this sense of belonging, and I remember wondering how he did it. We toured New York City performing in all five boroughs.

Sports were another big part of my life. I loved basketball but never thought I'd make the team but tried out anyway. It was a lark. But to my surprise, I did as a senior. I barely played in the exhibition games, and eventually, the coach pulled me aside and told me straight: "Cuneo, you're not gonna play much."

Instead of quitting, I jumped at the chance when he offered me the job of team manager. That turned out to be a great experience. I kept statistics, traveled with the team, and still felt like part of it. Funny enough, keeping stats gave me a little power; players would come over to check their points and rebounds during games.

It taught me something important: leadership isn't always about being the star on the court. Sometimes it's about stepping into a role where you can still make a difference.

At that same time, I was a decent Boy Scout, not an Eagle Scout, but I enjoyed it. Scouting taught me discipline, adventure, and gave me early glimpses of leadership in action.

High school, though, was where I really started to learn about myself. One thing became clear, and it's still true today: I'm highly driven when I'm interested in something, but when I'm not, I'm a complete zero.

This pattern frustrated my teachers. They'd tell me I wasn't living up to my potential, and looking back, they were right. But I couldn't force passion where none existed.

I carried that lesson with me as I started thinking about college. Since I was strong in math and science, a family friend suggested I look at Alfred University, known for its ceramic engineering program. I had mixed feelings. Alfred was three hundred miles from New York City, near the Pennsylvania border, practically in the middle of nowhere. Given everything going on at home, I wasn't sure I wanted to leave. But my mother insisted. She made me promise to go, believing I'd learn more about life away from the city than staying local.

My First Successful Turnaround

When I visited Alfred with my father, I fell in love with the place. It wasn't the academics—though I ended up majoring in glass science—it was the campus, the community, the atmosphere. It just felt right.

But once I got there, I struggled. For three years, I bounced on and off academic probation. I didn't manage my time well. In high school, I'd barely dated. Now I overcompensated; too much dating, a fraternity, endless hours in the pool hall, anything to escape the guilt I felt for leaving home.

During summers, I chased adventure. One summer, I became a certified scuba diver at the local YMCA and spent the season diving in the Finger Lakes, mostly retrieving outboard motors people had dropped off their boats. Sometimes, we'd spot old Indian canoes on the lake floor. It was simple, but it fed my need to escape.

Later, I got one of the most valuable summer jobs I ever had thanks to my grandfather Frank, a fill-in position at an exclusive apartment building on the Upper East Side. I rotated between doorman, handyman, and garbage man, covering for the men on vacation. They were all older immigrants— Scots, Germans, Italians, Irish—and working alongside them taught me more about people, hard work, and humility than any classroom ever could. They became quiet mentors, shaping how I understood leadership at the ground level.

If you asked anyone who knew me at Alfred University in the early '60s whether I was bound for any kind of success, let alone leadership, I'm not sure you'd get many optimistic answers. I was, to put it kindly, a screwup. Not a troublemaker exactly, but I wasn't focused or driven, and I certainly wasn't setting the world on fire academically.

But here's the thing about screwups: if you're lucky, or stubborn, you get a second act. Alfred was mine. I left school for a year when my father was sick, then came back and had two really good years.

During that year off working in New York, I grew up fast; probably matured five years in one. I started taking things seriously, and for the first time, everything began to click. By senior year, I was an officer in my fraternity, earned much of my tuition promoting rock and roll concerts, and made the dean's list. Funny how that happens. I graduated in 1967.

What's even funnier is that, years later, I'd return to Alfred, not as a nostalgic alum, but as a board member. Eventually, I became chairman of the board. They even gave me two honorary doctorates. Apparently, I'm the only person who's received two from Alfred.

Every time I went back to campus, especially for reunions, I could see the looks on my old classmates' faces. They were trying to place me. "That can't be *him*, the screwup, can it?" It was like watching someone see a ghost. And I loved that.

Because it proved a point I've come to believe deeply: you can screw up early in life and still come out ahead, *if* you're willing to change. I did. Alfred taught me that. It was my first turnaround: me.

After graduation, a job as a quality control engineer in a fiberglass plant offered stability and respectability. It was fine—on paper. But within a year, restlessness kicked in. That old "adventure gene" was flaring up again. A desk job didn't suit me, and settling down wasn't in the cards—not yet.

The Navy Helps Me Set a New Course

As I mentioned, my father had served in the navy. So had my uncle, who fought in the Battle of Leyte Gulf with Gen. Douglas MacArthur in 1944. I'd grown up watching black and white John Wayne war movies, romanticizing service, action, purpose. Maybe it sounds naïve, but that's what drew me in. I applied to Officer Candidate School.

They rejected me.

My first reaction was what you might expect: disappointment, maybe a little embarrassment. But then another voice kicked in, the one that said, *try again*. I wrote a letter directly to the Secretary of the Navy. I laid out my test scores, my family's service history, and most of all, my *intent*. This was the height of the Vietnam War. While others were dodging the draft, I was asking to serve. A month later, I got a letter back: I was in.

There's a lesson there I've carried with me ever since: When it matters, take the shot, even if you don't think you'll make it.

I reported to Officer Candidate School and poured myself into the work. I wasn't just motivated; I was on fire. I made cadet officer, graduated in the top 10 percent of my class, and chose destroyers in the Pacific. I wanted to be out there, at sea, in motion, in the middle of something bigger than myself. I was naïve about war, never thinking I could get hurt.

On that first tour, I was assigned to the USS *Joseph Strauss*, a guided missile destroyer. My first role? Damage Control Assistant, the lowest officer position on the ship. Before I even stepped aboard, I went through firefighting school in San Francisco. Haight-Ashbury was in full swing with the hippie movement. Long hair, folk music, and anti-war protests all around me. I stood out like a sore thumb: short hair, navy uniform, and absolutely no idea what I was walking into.

Eventually, I boarded the ship, via helicopter from an aircraft carrier, no less. They literally strapped me into a harness and dropped me onto the stern. That's how my navy career began.

The captain told me something on day one I've never forgotten: "You don't know anything yet. Watch, ask questions, learn." That humility, *that permission to not know*, was the foundation of everything that followed.

The ship saw real combat, once under fire from North Vietnamese shore batteries, bracketed by shells, facing close calls that bonded all aboard. Our crew, three hundred enlisted men and twenty officers from every background imaginable, didn't fight for politics or the flag. We fought for each other. Because in war, you don't survive alone.

That's where I first saw leadership at its rawest. Some led with courage, some not, some rose above their own prejudices. On that ship, I witnessed the power of shared purpose, the collapse of racial barriers, and the quiet strength that comes from empathy, clarity, and action under pressure.

Many of those moments, and the leaders, good and bad, who shaped them, will reappear throughout this book as I explore the Essentials of Superhero Leadership they revealed in real time.

When my time in the navy was up, I didn't want to leave. I loved it. But my wife made it clear: if I stayed in, I'd be doing it alone. Six months at sea, every year, for the rest of our lives? That wasn't what she'd signed up for. So, I made the hardest choice I'd made up to that point: I left.

But the navy wasn't done shaping me. Before I left, my captain—a man I'd only known a few months—said something that would change everything.

"You should go to Harvard Business School," he said.

I laughed. "I'm not Ivy League material," I told him.

And then he looked me dead in the eye and said, "Cuneo, you don't know how good you are."

That line became my compass. Whenever I've doubted myself, and I still do, I go back to that moment.

I sent in the application, took the test, and got in.

Finding My Footing at Harvard

I'll admit it, I didn't think I belonged at Harvard Business School. On registration day, I looked around and thought, *These people are geniuses. What the hell am I doing here?* Call it imposter syndrome, call it doubt, but it was real.

Most of my classmates had come straight from undergraduate school. They were twenty-one, maybe twenty-two. I was twenty-seven, had worked in a fiberglass plant, and done two tours in

Vietnam. I had stories and scars. And most importantly, I had perspective. The curriculum was based on class participation, and I had a lot to say. That difference gave me an unexpected edge.

I stayed with it—and something unexpected happened. As the months rolled by, I wasn't just holding my own, I was thriving. I was elected president of the International Business Club and achieved academic honors.

As graduation neared, the hot jobs were in investment banking and consulting. Everyone was scrambling to land offers at the most prestigious firms. But I knew myself well enough by then to recognize those weren't for me. The idea of sitting at a desk crunching numbers or flying city to city pitching investments didn't spark anything in me. Once again, that old adventurer gene kicked in—I wanted something more dynamic, more hands on.

But life isn't always a straight line. I still needed to earn a living, and the most accessible path, at least at the start, was corporate finance. So, I took a job at W.R. Grace, then moved to Bristol Myers. The opportunities were solid and diverse. The experiences taught me how to understand many different businesses by first analyzing the numbers and how they flowed.

At Bristol Myers, I became controller of a major division responsible for household names like Bufferin and Excedrin. Later, I was promoted to CFO of a group of six consumer companies, including Clairol.

It was a steady rise, but I was restless to be a general manager. I didn't know it yet, but I was setting the stage for the part of my career that would define me: turnarounds.

My First Real Test

My next assignment was as executive vice president for finance and manufacturing at Clairol's appliance division.

Within the company, the job wasn't considered glamorous, and to be honest, most of my peers saw it as a dead-end assignment. They told me flat out: *Take this job and you're finished here.*

But I couldn't help myself. The challenge called to me. It was messy, unpredictable—but right in my emotional wheelhouse. I took the leap.

The turning point came in 1983, when out of the blue, I was asked to take over the international appliance division. That meant hot rollers, curling irons, foot spas, the stuff that sold well in the US, but could struggle overseas.

The division was based in London, so I started commuting from New York to Europe almost monthly, figuring things out on the fly.

At first, I felt in over my head. I didn't see myself as a person with the skills for a turnaround. For the first six months, I was in a fog doubting myself, wondering if I'd made a career mistake. But then the fog began to lift. Slowly, the numbers started to improve.

I discovered bright, talented people who had been overlooked. I gave them room to run, encouraged them, backed their ideas. One of them, Fiona Harrison, would go on to run the entire international division. She was brilliant, and held back for too long.

We also changed how we approached product development. Instead of forcing US ideas on foreign markets, we started listening to our local international teams. A French woman wasn't going to wear hot rollers in public, period. But they had other ideas that could work, and we turned them into marketable products. In fact, we started bringing some of those European ideas back to the US and they sold very well.

That turnaround taught me the core of what would become my leadership philosophy: listen, empower, and move fast.

The Risk That Paid Off

That international turnaround led to another promotion, this time to lead the entire Clairol appliance division. Now I had full P&L responsibility for a $125 million business. It wasn't just about keeping things afloat. It was about growth, marketing, innovation. And guess what? The US business needed help too, and we got it done.

I'd gone from being a behind-the-scenes finance guy to a business leader, one who could actually drive results. And people noticed. Before long, Bristol Myers promoted me again, this time to run their Canadian pharmaceutical and nutrition business. It was a prestigious job, one that signaled big things ahead.

But here's the thing: I was bored. This was not a turnaround.

The team I inherited was outstanding. The numbers were strong. The business practically ran itself. I wasn't building anything. I wasn't fixing anything. I was just . . . managing. And I realized then that I didn't want to climb the corporate ladder for its own sake. I didn't want the cushy corner office if it meant dying of boredom. Having tasted the thrill of a turnaround, and becoming addicted to problem solving, I couldn't go back to a "normal" management job.

So I walked away.

The Lesson in Getting Fired

Next, I landed at Black & Decker. But I made a mistake. I was in a hurry to change jobs and didn't do my homework. On paper, the role was impressive: I was a group executive overseeing six divisions, but it didn't take long to realize that the company's culture didn't fit my leadership style. I also discovered that the company's due diligence leading up to a recent acquisition had been insufficient, particularly regarding the synergies Black & Decker expected to realize from the deal. I did everything I could to make it work, but the synergies simply weren't there. And in hindsight, I have to own the fact that I didn't do my own due diligence either. I saw the opportunity, moved too quickly, and ignored some warning signs. I regretted joining the company almost immediately.

There was nothing wrong with Black & Decker or its culture—it just wasn't a place where someone like me, a guy from the streets of New York, was going to thrive in the long term. I wasn't going to be popular with that leadership team, and I knew it. After two years on the job, I got fired. My business results were solid, but this was the one time in my career where the cultural misalignment—and my own misjudgment—cost me the job.

But I have no regrets. Because by then, I'd figured out my calling: this is what I do. I take on the hard jobs, fix broken businesses, and try to bring out the best in people. Turnarounds weren't just something I *could* do; they were what I was *meant* to do.

And getting let go? That just cleared the way for the next big challenge: Remington, and then ultimately Marvel.

Remington was a well-known men's grooming brand when I stepped in as CEO, but the business was challenged by outdated products, sagging sales, and no clear direction. The board brought me in to change that.

We tightened operations, cut unnecessary costs, launched new advertising, and reinvested in product development. I was proud of the progress. The business was stabilizing, and a clear path forward was emerging. I then acquired my former Clairol appliance business from Bristol Myers, creating a unified company offering both men's and women's beauty grooming products. Sales doubled, and we eventually sold the business to a private equity firm.

I stayed on to allow the buyer to find someone to replace me, and I walked away . . . *again.*

Next, I had a short stint with a small private equity firm based in New York. But it was a temporary situation while I was still looking for the next big turnaround. That's when I got the call. It was from the chairman of Marvel who I knew from Remington's board.

Marvel had just come out of a brutal two-year bankruptcy battle between Carl Icahn and Ike Perlmutter. Ike had won. And now, they needed a CEO. Someone who could steer the ship, rebuild confidence, and make sense of a business that had been gutted and demoralized.

I don't think I'd read a Marvel comic book in my life. I didn't know the difference between Thor and Thanos or the first thing about comic book art. But what I *did* know was the art of the turnaround. So, I asked for a week to dig in.

Marvel was still trading publicly, even through bankruptcy, so I could access all the financials. And what jumped out at me, what completely hooked me, was this: they had 4,700 characters in their IP portfolio. Some only appeared once, some we all knew like Spider-Man, the Hulk, Captain America, but the portfolio had been valued at $500 million coming out of bankruptcy. I remember thinking: *Spider-Man alone is worth that, if you do it right.*

So I said yes.

The first year was hell. The stock dropped from seven dollars to two dollars. Our CFO quit, perhaps convinced we were heading for another bankruptcy. I couldn't afford to replace him, so I took on the additional CFO role myself. That meant I was closer to the numbers than ever before, maybe closer than any CEO in Marvel history. Today, you couldn't get away with that dual role under Sarbanes-Oxley rules. But back then? It gave me a front-row seat to every lever I had to pull.

We clawed our way back. We licensed our best characters into video games, opened new streams of licensing revenue, and, critically, I strengthened leadership in publishing. I wasn't going to let ego, favoritism, or tunnel vision keep Marvel from attracting the best creative talent. That's when we brought in Joe Quesada, a highly respected comic book artist and editor, to lead publishing, a major shift that paid off. We were on the brink of something big, but we still had to execute.

I was privileged to work alongside some remarkable people during my time at Marvel—true visionaries who played a pivotal role in what became one of the most successful corporate turnarounds in modern business history.

Ike Perlmutter, the principal shareholder of Marvel, was an intense, deeply focused businessman. Avi Arad was the driving force behind our early success in films. Then there was David Maisel, whose vision quite literally launched Marvel Studios.

It was a defining moment, not just in my career, but in the world of corporate reinvention. If I had to describe it in Marvel terms, we assembled our own Avengers of Turnaround Leadership. Every person had their superpower.

We drove revenue growth, cut costs, and took strategic leaps that fundamentally changed the business. Just ten years after emerging from bankruptcy, we sold Marvel to Disney in 2009 for $4.5 billion.

Together, we didn't just save a company. We helped launch a global cultural and cinematic phenomenon.

During my time as CEO of Marvel, I was asked to give a speech on leadership. I was nervous; I'd never really spoken publicly about my leadership philosophy before. So, during an eleven-hour flight to China, I started jotting down the lessons I'd learned over the years. Not theory. Not buzzwords. Just what had worked. What hadn't. Where I'd failed. What I'd seen in war, in business, in life.

By the time I landed, there were twenty-eight leadership essentials scribbled down.

Those essentials became the foundation of everything I would go on to teach, mentor, and speak about.

They didn't just sit on a list—they became my toolkit. My version of Iron Man's workshop. Yes, I first relied on them in turnaround situations, where the stakes were high and the path uncertain. But over time, I saw how these essentials applied far beyond crisis moments. They've guided me—and others—through all kinds of leadership challenges: building teams, making bold decisions, mentoring emerging leaders, and navigating everyday complexities. These are not just principles for saving a company—they're principles for leading one.

So here I am, decades later, still working, still chairing boards, still learning. Still dreaming. Because that's the truth about leadership: it doesn't stop. If you think it does, you're finished. I'm still figuring out where I need to grow, where I need to listen better, where I need to "reverse mentor" with the younger generation. I've learned that leadership isn't just for the top of the org chart—it affects every single one of us. At work. At home. In the world we share.

That's why I'm writing this book. To pass on what I've learned, not in theory, but in action. To share the scars and the wins. To help you find the leader in yourself, or to recognize the kind of leadership worth following.

Because one thing I know for sure: leadership is more of an art than a science, and like every great superhero story, it's a journey of purpose, growth, and grit that never truly ends. And if you do it right, the legacy you leave isn't just in what you build, but in the heroes you help create along the way.

GENERATE POSITIVE ENERGY FROM MINUTE ONE!

When I joined Marvel Entertainment as CEO in 1999, I stepped into what could only be described as a critical survival situation. Fresh out of bankruptcy, the company was weighed down by high-yield debt.

Our stock eventually plummeted to a mere ninety-six cents per share. It was an undeniable low point for a company that owned some of the most beloved characters in the world.

Walking into the offices that first day, the atmosphere was suffocating, reminiscent of a locker room where a team hadn't won a game all season. Tomorrow, they'd face the league champions, and here I was, the new coach they hardly knew and barely hoped could make a difference.

This company was my team now, and the game was survival. In both cases, winning had felt out of reach for far too long. The empty stands and harsh press weren't just about lost games or money—it was the weariness of repeated failure that had drained the spirit out of the place.

You could feel it the moment you walked in. The office was silent—not in a calm way, but in a way that pressed down on you.

Each empty cubicle, each echo in the hallway, told a story of people who'd given up hope.

The employees I met tried to smile, but it didn't reach their eyes. They were guarded, polite, and clearly bracing for another disappointment. From the looks I got—wary, tired eyes—I could tell they saw me as just the latest in a long line of would-be saviors.

They'd been through it all: layoffs, bankruptcies, good people packing up and leaving. Investors had bailed. Customers stopped picking up the phone. And every time it rang, it felt like bad news calling again.

The challenge was massive. We didn't just need to fix the finances—we had to rebuild trust, reignite morale, and prove this company was still worth believing in.

Managing wouldn't be enough. This would take leadership—with vision, purpose, and relentless follow-through. We needed a strategy that wouldn't just stop the bleeding, but actually push us forward. And to me, that started with something everyone else seemed to be overlooking: Marvel's incredible intellectual properties. The characters were iconic, but they weren't being used to their full potential.

At times, I caught myself wishing I could call on the superheroes themselves. Each one of them had traits I needed on my team: Spider-Man's instinct to connect with people, Iron Man's technological brilliance, Wolverine's grit, Hulk's strength balanced with smarts, and the X-Men's ability to pull together, despite being wildly different.

Those qualities would've come in handy. Because I was about to lead one of the toughest turnarounds of my career.

And I knew one thing right away: constant communication would be critical. I couldn't afford to be distant—not when everyone was watching so closely, looking for any sign that nothing had really changed. I quickly learned that every gesture, every word, mattered. More than I ever realized.

I remember one moment, during a previous turnaround, that drove this lesson home. It was a hectic morning—I was distracted by a tangle of personal issues—and I walked right past our receptionist without offering my usual cheerful hello. She'd been with the company for thirty years. A steady, kind presence. The kind of person who had quietly weathered every storm that place had seen.

But that small oversight—just a missed greeting—was enough to rattle her. She thought I was signaling that layoffs were coming. By midday, the rumor mill was in full swing, and I was scrambling to put out fires I hadn't meant to start.

That incident hit me hard. It showed me how powerful presence really is. Something as simple as a friendly nod or hello can mean the difference between calm and chaos. That morning reminded me that when trust is fragile, even the smallest actions carry outsized meaning.

From that day on, I made a conscious effort to stay "up" whenever I was visible to the team. I wanted my words—and just as importantly, my body language—to project hope and confidence. As a leader, I couldn't afford even a flicker of doubt. People were watching, looking for reassurance in every smile, every nod.

Even small gestures, like hosting a spontaneous pizza party, took on new meaning. They weren't just breaks from the grind—they became chances for open, honest conversation.

During those informal gatherings, I encouraged the team to share their fears and concerns. One lunch in particular stands out: I spoke candidly about our situation, and explained how we could turn our challenges into stepping stones. Everyone had a role to play in the turnaround—and they needed to hear that.

Honesty became my default. I didn't sugarcoat the problems. To do so would've insulted the intelligence of people who'd lived through the worst of it. Instead, I was direct: the road ahead would be tough, but it was navigable—and we'd walk it together.

"Yes, we have serious problems," I would say in meetings. "But together, we can—and will—overcome them."

At Marvel, the plan I laid out centered on a few critical actions. First, we had to unlock the full value of our character portfolio—by rebuilding relationships with film studios and merchandisers that had been neglected. We renegotiated deals, pursued new partnerships, and pushed to showcase the untapped potential of our IP.

Second, we needed to restructure our debt. That meant working closely with financial advisors to create some breathing room—so we could reinvest in what mattered most: creative talent, marketing, and future growth.

Just as crucial was reigniting the creative spark that made Marvel special in the first place. I made it a point to spend time with our creative teams, listening to their ideas and encouraging them to keep dreaming big.

The first *X-Men* movie was already in production when I arrived, and it felt like the perfect starting point—a signal that our characters still had enormous power to connect with audiences.

We greenlit new projects—not just in traditional comics, but across digital and multimedia platforms that could reach new generations of fans. By partnering with major studios, we began laying the foundation for what would become Marvel's cinematic resurgence.

Around six months in, I found myself thinking of Marvel in terms of a wagon wheel. At the center—the hub—was our treasure chest of intellectual property: more than seven thousand characters. The spokes represented all the ways we could monetize that IP. The rim? That was the synergy between those spokes.

The problem was, the wheel was wobbly. Only one and a half spokes were really working. Our comic book publishing division was solid. But our licensing efforts—where the real opportunity lay—were disjointed and underdeveloped. A broken spoke, if you will.

We had to fix that. My vision was to strengthen each spoke—and build real connections between them. I wanted a system where every spoke supported the others. So that a fan who came in through one door—say, a movie—would naturally discover the rest: games, toys, comics, you name it. That kind of synergy would become our engine for growth.

One of my first major moves was striking a partnership with Activision—just three months after I arrived. We agreed to develop video games based on some of our biggest characters, including Spider-Man. This deal didn't just add a new spoke; it helped reinforce the licensing arm, integrating it more deeply with the rest of the business.

The transformational moment came about a year later, with the release of *X-Men*. That film's success wasn't just about box office numbers—it unlocked a powerful new spoke: motion picture licensing.

The impact was so strong, we had to break that spoke into several more. Toys, costumes, merchandise—each became a robust revenue stream in its own right.

By the end of my first year, what had once been a shaky wheel had become a powerful engine—with five strong, interdependent spokes. Each one supported and amplified the others, creating a self-sustaining cycle of growth and innovation. That didn't just stabilize the business—it moved the stock price from under a dollar to levels that finally reflected our potential.

The framework helped us identify what was broken and where to apply pressure. And it worked. We began attracting top-tier talent, people who saw what was happening and wanted in. Their energy and expertise helped accelerate everything we'd started.

What had once felt like a company in survival mode now buzzed with belief. People were leaning in, not looking for the exits. That shift, from fear to hope, was the real win.

For me, it was a powerful reminder: turnarounds aren't just about numbers, they're about people. You have to believe in the value that's already there, even if others can't see it yet. At Marvel, that meant reanimating dormant assets like licensing and consumer products, building momentum one working spoke at a time. But none of that would have happened without a mindset shift, positivity, projected and shared. When people start to believe again, creativity flows, energy returns, and progress accelerates. And at Marvel, we were just getting started.

ESSENTIAL #2

BE HUMAN. BE HONEST. TELL PEOPLE WHAT YOU THINK. ADMIT YOUR MISTAKES

As a young naval officer during the Vietnam War, I witnessed leadership in one of the most demanding environments imaginable. My service aboard the USS *Joseph Strauss*—a guided missile destroyer stationed just twenty miles off the North Vietnamese coast—didn't just accelerate my education in leadership. It fundamentally shaped how I would lead for the rest of my life.

The *Strauss* displaced 6,000 tons, stretched 437 feet long and 47 feet wide, with a 20-foot draft. She was home to three hundred sailors and twenty officers. Our mission was plane guarding—stationing ourselves one nautical mile in front of or behind the aircraft carrier to rescue any navy pilots forced to ditch their planes in the water.

I had the midwatch, from midnight to 4 a.m., when we operated under "darkened ship" conditions. That meant all exterior lights were off—except for faint red lights along the deck—making us nearly invisible to both enemies and allies.

Alone on the bridge, just a month into my career, I was responsible for reporting our bearing and range relative to the carrier and the other destroyers in our group. It was a high-pressure role with zero room for error.

The captain, a seasoned and respected leader, ran the ship from the bridge almost around the clock. He ate there. He even slept there. Watching him lead from the front—always present, always calm—left a lasting impression on me.

One night, around 2 a.m., that impression would be tested.

Amid the quiet tension of the midwatch, we received orders to adjust our position behind the aircraft carrier, which was turning into the wind to recover aircraft. The captain, momentarily asleep in his chair, was awakened by the movement and hushed chatter on the bridge as the Officer of the Deck (OOD) calculated the necessary changes in course and speed.

The OOD holds one of the most critical roles aboard a navy ship—responsible for safe navigation and command execution during their watch. It requires constant vigilance, confident decision-making, and a deep grasp of every operational aspect of the vessel.

Still groggy, the captain insisted on rechecking the OOD's calculations. Roused from sleep and disoriented, he countermanded the order and issued a new course. The shift in atmosphere was immediate. Silent glances passed between the watch team—no one said a word, but their concern was palpable.

Moments later, the stillness was shattered. A destroyer appeared out of the darkness, closing fast on our starboard side. We were on a collision course—two warships converging at a combined speed of 64 knots (about 73 mph).

The captain snapped to action, ordering a hard-right rudder. The ship groaned into the turn. But the *Strauss* didn't just pivot— at 437 feet and 6,000 tons, it continued to surge forward, even as the bow began to swing. It was like a car hitting black ice: you can steer, but the momentum still carries you ahead. Our stern narrowly cleared the other ship's bow.

It was a close call. Too close.

You could see the faint glow of red walkway lights on the other ship's deck—just thirty feet away. A surreal, almost silent reminder of how close we'd come. I remember thinking, *There's no way we're getting out of this mess alive.*

The captain's initial miscalculation had brought us to the brink, but his quick, decisive handling of the ship pulled us back from disaster. While 95 percent of the crew slept through the event, those of us on the bridge stood frozen in a brief but gripping moment of fear, followed by a flood of relief as the danger passed.

Despite the gravity of the mistake, what stood out most was the captain's responsiveness under pressure. There was no time to second-guess. He acted fast and with clarity. That too is leadership.

There was no dramatic debrief that night. We returned to our stations and completed our operations with a sharper edge and quiet gratitude that we were still afloat.

By morning, the corridors of the *Strauss* buzzed with whispered speculation. In close quarters, word of a near-miss spreads fast. The story was already reshaping into a shared understanding: the captain had made a serious error that had nearly cost us everything.

He didn't let that version go unanswered.

Later that day, the captain convened all available officers—except those on watch—for a meeting. That alone was unusual. What followed was even more so: honesty.

In a calm, measured voice, he began, "Last night I made a mistake, and we must all study it and learn from it so we avoid this situation in the future."

This wasn't just a briefing. It was a methodical, transparent breakdown of what had happened. For the next hour, we examined every decision, every command, and the chain of execution. The captain didn't deflect responsibility. He owned it—and used it as a teaching moment.

In the hypermasculine, often stoic culture of the military during the Vietnam War era, that kind of candor was rare. At the time, military leaders were expected to project infallibility—authority unquestioned, vulnerability unseen. But history has shown that the most respected leaders are those who can admit their flaws and learn from their missteps.

What could have undermined his authority had the opposite effect. His willingness to be accountable only deepened the crew's respect. It was clear his priority wasn't his image—it was our safety, and the integrity of the ship's command.

That moment changed how I saw him. The man I'd doubted the night before had, through humility and courage, earned my loyalty for the rest of my naval career. It taught me one of the most pivotal lessons in leadership: true authority doesn't come from projecting perfection—it comes from owning responsibility and showing commitment to those you lead.

Years later, he was promoted to rear admiral. The navy, clearly, had recognized the strength behind his leadership style.

And that lesson followed me into civilian life. In business, similar dynamics play out every day. When a CEO is focused solely on the stock price—especially when their compensation is tied to it—employees quickly recognize that personal gain has taken priority over the company's long-term health. That erodes trust and loyalty.

By contrast, leaders who consistently put the well-being of the company—and their people—first foster a culture of trust, stability, and shared purpose. Teams under these leaders don't just comply—they commit. They stay. They strive. Because they know they're being led by someone who values their future as much as their own.

Strong leaders don't use authority to instill fear or assert dominance. They use it to create an environment of respect—built through transparency, honesty, and accountability. They show their humanity. They acknowledge mistakes, learn from them, and, when needed, make amends. Especially in a turnaround, where morale is low and trust has been fractured, these qualities aren't just helpful, they're essential.

That's what our captain demonstrated. By owning his error and turning it into a shared learning moment, he didn't just avert a crisis—he deepened the crew's trust and strengthened our cohesion.

That same approach applies in business, where aligning diverse teams toward a common goal demands not just strategic clarity, but emotional integrity.

Looking back, both in the navy and in the boardroom, the lesson is unmistakable: the most effective leaders act not in service of their own image or rewards, but in service of their people and their mission. They create environments where loyalty is earned, performance thrives, and transformation becomes possible.

They don't lead from above, they lead alongside. And that makes all the difference.

It brings to mind Captain America, not the icon in red, white, and blue, but Steve Rogers, the man underneath the shield. In *Captain America: Civil War*, when confronted with the fallout of his decisions and the consequences of unchecked power, Steve doesn't deflect. He listens. He takes responsibility. And when he realizes he was wrong about Tony Stark's parents and Bucky's involvement, he owns it, not with excuses, but with a handwritten letter: *"I'm sorry . . . I was wrong about you. The truth is, I'm not sure if it's worth it if I'm the only one standing."*

That's what leadership looks like: not a flawless figure at the front of the line, but a human being willing to be vulnerable, to admit misjudgments, and to rebuild trust through action.

Like my captain aboard the *Strauss*, Steve Rogers didn't lead through bravado or unshakable certainty. He led through moral courage, the kind that says, *I'll take the hit if it means protecting my team.* The kind that doesn't just inspire loyalty, but earns it. Because in war, in business, or on the bridge of a destroyer in the middle of the night, people don't follow perfection.

They follow character.

And if you're trying to lead a company, a culture, or even your own life, character is where you start.

Because the next test of leadership doesn't always come with a warning.

But it always comes.

ESSENTIAL #3

COMMUNICATE CONSISTENT MESSAGES: WALK THE TALK

In the previous chapter, I shared how a captain's willingness to admit a mistake earned my lifelong respect—and taught me how powerful honesty can be in leadership.

But being honest once isn't enough. If you want people to trust you over time, you have to follow through—say what you mean, and do what you say. That's where consistency comes in. This next essential is about walking the talk. Because if honesty builds trust, consistency keeps it alive. And that starts with how we communicate.

When I was twenty-four years old, just starting out as a young officer in the navy aboard the guided missile destroyer USS *Joseph Strauss* during the Vietnam War, I learned a lesson that stayed with me for life: the power of clear, consistent communication.

The captains I served under excelled at it. There was never confusion among the crew. All three hundred sailors and twenty officers knew our mission, what was expected of us, and the risks and rewards.

These captains used the ship's loudspeaker system to keep us informed—about our objectives, our presence, even when we were under attack. I'll never forget one moment during general quarters: the captain calmly came over the speaker to tell us that North Vietnamese shore batteries had fired on us, we'd returned fire, and no one was hurt. That mix of real-time updates and steady, strategic clarity built trust—and confidence.

After two tours in Vietnam, I carried that model into the business world. But not every leader shared it. Many withheld information, thinking secrecy gave them control. In my experience, it did the opposite. It bred confusion, mistrust, and frustration.

I've always leaned toward overcommunicating—sometimes to a fault. But if there's one thing I've learned, it's this: consistent communication is essential. In formal settings, that might mean company-wide emails, town halls, or global livestreams.

Just as vital is informal communication. I like to walk the office floor, speak with people one-on-one or in small groups. In factories or warehouses, I try to walk alone—no entourage. When it's just me, people relax and open up, especially about difficult topics. These moments provide what I call "bullet intelligence," raw, honest insights that can guide action, as long as they're verified.

People appreciate being asked about themselves. These small conversations build trust and make tougher conversations easier. That trust doesn't appear from thin air. It comes from visible, engaged leadership.

In a turnaround, that means showing up, consistently. Fear of job loss, change, or company collapse is real, and the antidote is constant, clear communication.

Turnarounds taught me this more than any other experience. The battlefield may be different, but the fear is the same. So is the remedy: communicate regularly and truthfully, whether the news is good or bad. That includes shaping culture, not just strategy. Real change starts with mindset, how people treat one another and how they show up for the company.

Culture change starts by naming the problem, pointing to where we're going, and how we'll get there. Vision is about answering a few essential questions:

- Where will we compete?
- How will we compete?
- How will we treat customers?
- How will we treat each other?
- What must we excel at—innovation, product development, operational efficiency, or something else?

It sounds simple, but clarity and consistency are hard. Misunderstandings happen. When I sensed confusion, I addressed it immediately to realign the team.

Trust is built two ways: through consistent messaging and through action. Leaders are always being watched—especially in a turnaround. Employees want honesty, even when it's tough. When asked about layoffs, I was always honest: yes, no, or "we're still evaluating." People preferred hard truth over vague reassurance.

Communication alone isn't enough. If your actions contradict your words, trust erodes. If they align, belief takes root—and belief is what drives change. But not everyone adapts. Some people simply don't belong in the culture you're building.

Take sexual harassment, for example. When it happens, act fast. Show you mean what you say. One salesperson made a sexist joke during a team meeting. I called him out immediately and later apologized to the team. He never did it again. That kind of visible accountability reinforces the culture.

But communication must remain consistent through every layer of the company. That's not easy. Sometimes messages get filtered—or twisted. When I saw people deliberately distorting my words, I acted. If it was a pattern, I removed them. In a turnaround, there's no room for "organizational cancer."

At one company, informal conversations revealed that a key executive—who also had equity in the business—was undermining me behind the scenes. I confronted him. He denied it. I made it clear that we couldn't work together unless he changed. To his credit, he did. That experience drove home the value of direct, informal communication. It shapes culture, builds trust, and gives people the clarity and confidence to move forward, even in uncertainty.

One last example: I once joined a multinational company where leadership kept touting the synergies between divisions. But they didn't exist. US customers wanted simple, affordable products. In Europe, one market prized precision and sophistication; another was deeply resistant to change. The assumption of alignment was pure fantasy. The real issue wasn't operational, it was cultural. And no one at the top had taken the time to really understand that.

Once we named the problem, we could fix it. We stopped pushing for uniformity and started empowering regional teams to tailor products and messaging to their markets. We built cross-cultural teams—not just to translate language, but to translate mindset. It wasn't about giving up on synergy—it was about redefining it. That's when results started to shift.

The lesson stuck with me: you can't lead what you don't take time to understand. Especially in complex, global organizations, leadership starts with listening. Assumptions get you stuck. Empathy and curiosity move you forward.

Consistency builds trust. When employees hear the same message in meetings, emails, and hallway conversations, they feel confident in leadership. But balance is key: be approachable, but don't let standards slip. One leader I admire for that balance is General George Patton. He led from the front. His troops respected him because he cared about them and demanded excellence.

Winston Churchill was another. During World War II, he refused to surrender—even when others pushed for negotiations with Nazi Germany. His most famous speech, *We will fight them on the beaches*, rallied an entire nation. What made Churchill so effective wasn't just his rhetoric—it was his willingness to listen, to show up, and to speak with clarity and conviction in the face of crisis.

I've always tried to lead in that spirit. Even when a company is on the brink of radical change, people want to be heard. You can't act on every suggestion, but if you show up, listen, and take meaningful action based on what you hear, you earn trust.

That's the power of consistent communication. It's not just about sending emails or hosting town halls. It's about aligning your words with your actions—every day, in every room you enter. That's what builds real culture. That's what makes people believe that change is not just possible, but already underway.

It's what the navy taught me early on: communication isn't just a tool—it's the foundation of leadership.

And in the Marvel universe, no one learned that lesson more painfully than Tony Stark.

In *Iron Man*, Stark begins as a brilliant but reckless weapons manufacturer—sharp with a soundbite, but blind to the ripple effects of his own actions. His company preached "peace through strength," while secretly profiting from conflict. That disconnect nearly killed him—and worse, it cost innocent lives. It wasn't until Stark saw the damage firsthand that he changed course. He didn't just stop making weapons—he became the weapon, suiting up to protect the very people he had once endangered.

But even after donning the armor, the real transformation wasn't in his tech—it was in his messaging. He went from deflecting responsibility to owning it. From hiding behind quips to standing in front of cameras and saying, *I am Iron Man*. That moment wasn't just iconic—it was consistent. He aligned his words with his mission and backed them up with action.

Of course, the journey wasn't perfect. Stark still stumbled, especially when his ego outpaced his empathy. But over time, he evolved into a leader who communicated not just with charisma, but with conviction. In *Endgame*, it's not just the suit that makes the impact—it's the trust he's earned by finally walking the talk.

That's what turns communication into credibility. And credibility into leadership. Even in a world of chaos, people will follow the voice they trust, especially when it's proven, again and again, to match the action.

But what happens when leadership means saying less—and listening more?

LISTEN EVEN IF YOU KNOW THE ANSWER

Constructive listening has become a lost art in leadership. We live in an era of nonstop information—emails, texts, alerts—where we skim for key points and miss the bigger picture. But when it comes to leading people, we can't afford to just react. We have to truly hear what's being said.

Personally, I've never really been a great listener—a flaw rooted deeply in my inherent lack of patience. This shortcoming has sometimes put a strain on my relationships, and I am constantly working to improve.

The COVID pandemic has only intensified these challenges, significantly altering the way we communicate. It's peculiar how, even when close enough to touch someone, screens often dominate our interactions.

Our eyes dart to notifications, our attention is split between Zoom, Microsoft Teams, and the real world, leaving little room for genuine connection. This relentless onslaught of digital interruptions makes it incredibly tough to maintain the focus needed for deep, meaningful conversations.

In leadership, the ability to truly listen—not just to the words but to grasp the entire message being conveyed—is absolutely invaluable. It's about absorbing the full context, understanding underlying tones, and reading between the lines, all of which are essential for truly effective leadership.

Reflecting on my own experiences, I've found that the most fruitful discussions often happen away from the glare of devices. Whether it's a strategic meeting in a quiet conference room or a casual chat over coffee, the real insights come from truly listening—not just to the words, but to the person. A glance, a hesitation, a shift in tone—these small signals often say more than the statement itself.

Even if I think I already know the answer, actively listening can reveal nuances and perspectives I might have missed or not fully appreciated. This approach not only deepens my understanding but also strengthens relationships, as it shows genuine respect for the other person's input and experiences.

Every day, whether I'm heading into New York on a train or sitting down for a meeting, I strive to bring genuine curiosity and openness into every interaction. This approach isn't just about making an impact, it's about fostering respect, deepening understanding, and growing personally, no matter your age or experience.

This mindset shift became particularly important after leaving the navy, where communication was direct and quick, focused primarily on efficiency. This method served well in the military, especially under high-pressure combat conditions requiring swift decision-making. However, transitioning this approach to the civilian sphere, especially in a corporate environment like at Bristol Myers, proved challenging.

I vividly remember one of my first major meetings at the company. Armed with confidence and a bit too eager to assert leadership, I found myself in a room with seasoned professionals ready to tackle complex issues with the thoughtful consideration they deserved. Yet there I was—interrupting, summarizing, and rushing through the meeting like it was a military debrief—before anyone had even finished making their point.

After the meeting, a respected colleague pulled me aside. His approach was kind but straightforward. "You've got good ideas," he said, "but you're not really listening to anyone else. It seems like you're here to broadcast your thoughts and not to receive any signals." That feedback hit hard, revealing that the directness I valued was perceived as brash and disrespectful in a corporate setting.

This experience was a critical pivot point, underscoring the need to adapt my approach to communication. It highlighted the importance of genuinely listening—not just hearing—as a means to respect and integrate the perspectives of others, thereby enriching both decision-making and interpersonal relationships. I was no longer at sea, where complex communications were a luxury as rare as good food.

It took time to adjust—and that lesson was reinforced during a surprisingly confrontational meeting sometime later at Bristol-Myers. My role as a vice president had led me to cultivate a self-image as a competent, respected leader. When my team assembled unexpectedly in my office one day, their serious expressions hinted at a significant issue. However, the emergency turned out to be about my own shortcomings.

They expressed their concerns candidly, explaining that it seemed I didn't value their input because I often dismissed their ideas before they had the chance to fully articulate them. This practice, they noted, made them feel undervalued and overlooked. In effect, I was answering my own questions—before they had the chance to.

Their honest feedback struck a nerve, and they were right. My approach often involved racing through discussions with a mental checklist, rarely pausing to consider their viewpoints thoroughly.

That day was a profound wake-up call, teaching me the immense value that active listening could bring to my leadership. Often, the insights from my team contained the keys to better outcomes—insights I had sometimes missed by not fully listening. It became clear that no single person could encompass every aspect of a situation alone.

This realization about the importance of listening in my professional life started to echo in my personal life as well. It's like wearing two different hats. At work, my impatience might drive efficiency, pushing projects forward swiftly. But at home, the dynamics are entirely different. Family life demands a kind of patience I've often struggled to summon.

My wife has always been a clear mirror for me in this regard. She's pointed out countless times at social gatherings, "You're talking too much. Let other people talk." She sees it clearly, even when I don't. It took me years to truly understand what she meant—not just to hear her words but to absorb them and reflect on them. In social settings, I realized, my eagerness to share my thoughts and stories often didn't leave much room for others to share theirs, a behavior I've been actively working to change.

This challenge wasn't just about exchanging information like in a meeting—it was about connection: bonding, sharing experiences, and, most importantly, listening. My wife's gentle nudges helped me see that true balance was needed—not just hearing others but allowing them the space to express themselves fully, which is what deepens relationships.

From these personal experiences, I learned that reclaiming the art of listening in an era rife with digital distractions starts with intention. We must consciously decide to prioritize the person in front of us, giving them our undivided attention.

Although it might seem like a small piece of the puzzle, actively listening has the power to profoundly enhance our communication skills and deepen our relationships, both personally and professionally. By embracing this approach, we not only improve our interactions but also lay the groundwork for a more connected and empathetic environment, whether in the boardroom or beyond. Even today, decades later, I make it a point before every meeting or key conversation to let others speak first.

This lesson became vividly clear to me during a product photo shoot at another company. Upon arriving, I initially thought the setup was all wrong and began to intervene. However, taking a moment to listen to the marketing team explain their rationale showed me that they were right. They had a deeper understanding of the goals for advertising content, and had carefully crafted their approach based on that expertise.

That day, I learned stepping back and trusting others isn't about losing control—it's about respect and realizing my way isn't the only way. That mindset not only improved the outcome of the photo shoot but also strengthened the team's trust and morale.

If there's one thing I've learned, it's this: recognizing the value and trust of your team is essential in leadership. When people feel respected and acknowledged, they're not just working for you—they're working with you.

To truly connect with your team, you have to genuinely see them—and listen. No matter how seasoned you are, you don't have all the answers. A great example of that mindset is Professor Charles Xavier from the X-Men. He values the unique perspectives and talents of every member of his team.

Xavier isn't just a leader—he can literally tap into people's thoughts and feelings. It makes him the ultimate listener. Imagine being able to hear not only what someone says, but what they hold back. His telepathy is a metaphor for leadership at its best: tuning in deeply, even when you think you already know the answer.

If we could all channel our inner Professor X during conversations, imagine the depth of understanding and connection we'd unlock.

Let's explore how we might enhance our listening skills to foster these richer, more meaningful interactions. Here are a few steps to start us on this path:

Step #1: Hold Back on Interrupting
Make a conscious effort not to cut people off mid-sentence. It's not just courteous—it's the foundation of real listening.

Step #2: Echo Their Points

Once they've finished speaking, reflect back what you heard. It shows you're engaged—and helps you both stay aligned.

Step #3: Dive Deeper with Questions

Even when you think you know the answer, ask a follow-up. It keeps the door open—and shows their input matters.

By integrating these steps into your daily interactions, you're not merely practicing good communication; you are actively building stronger, more empathetic connections with those around you. This shift in how you engage with others can significantly transform your role from simply being a boss to becoming a true leader.

Embracing the mindset that you can learn from others and valuing the collective intelligence of your team are key to this transformation. The best leaders don't just direct, they listen, learn, and grow alongside their teams. That's how transformation happens.

This approach isn't just about being nice; it's about being effective and leveraging every resource at your disposal to its fullest potential. And one of the most underused resources? Listening. Not passive hearing, but real, engaged, constructive listening.

ESSENTIAL #5

AVOID PREJUDICES AND EMBRACE DIVERSITY

Of all the lessons in leadership that apply to both business and life, avoiding prejudice is one of the most far-reaching and valuable.

In my seven corporate turnarounds, I've seen firsthand how critical it is to adapt. Leadership fundamentals may stay the same, but the tactics and approaches always need to evolve to fit the specific challenges at hand. Sometimes, those challenges stem directly from bias within an organization—bias that not only hinders progress but also damages morale.

At one of my companies, a senior vice president overseeing a growing business unit started expanding his team. At first, it seemed like things were running smoothly, but it didn't take long to notice a problem. His hiring decisions were clearly biased—he only brought in people who shared his religion, leaving no room for diversity.

Even though his team performed well, that bias had a ripple effect on the broader organization. Employees outside his group began to feel stuck, knowing they had little chance of moving into this high-growth area because they weren't of the "right" faith. Over time, what could have been a collaborative, integrated unit turned into a cultural island, completely isolated from the rest of the company.

Dealing with this wasn't easy—I had to respect the sensitivities around his religion while fixing a problem that was hurting the entire company. Balancing those challenges took some careful steps, but it had to be done. I'll share how I handled it a little later in this chapter.

Looking back, it's clear that the values instilled during childhood shaped my approach to situations like this. Growing up in a home where prejudice wasn't tolerated—thanks to parents and grandparents who emphasized fairness and respect—left a lasting impression.

They never spoke badly about anyone because of their race, religion, background, or education. They looked at people as individuals, nothing more, nothing less.

Growing up in the diverse neighborhood of Flushing, Queens, we were surrounded by a mix of cultures. Living in an environment as diverse as New York City meant you had to adapt, blend in, and learn to respect differences just to get by. Even in high school, where cliques were everywhere, I felt at ease moving between groups and never stuck to just one.

Stepping into the "real world" was the first time bias became impossible to ignore, raising questions about how anyone could hold negative feelings toward someone they didn't even know. Biases—whether against people or ideas—often seem rooted in insecurities that cloud judgment and, in the end, hold people back from achieving success.

The same goes for business. A leader with strong prejudices often makes bad decisions because their emotions and assumptions get in the way. In today's connected, global world, being open-minded isn't just a nice-to-have—it's essential. Success requires embracing different cultures, ideas, and approaches.

Bias rears its ugly head in all kinds of ways, and as leaders, it's on us to make sure it doesn't undermine our organizations. Whether it's tied to class, religion, education, or gender, prejudice often hides in what seem like harmless comments, such as, "People from that country don't make good partners." These attitudes don't just hurt morale—they also hold back growth and collaboration.

By staying aware of bias and building a culture of respect and acceptance, leaders can help their organizations thrive in today's diverse and fast-changing world.

In today's age of progressive values, blatant discrimination in the US has often gone underground, hidden behind polite words or subtle actions. While that might look like progress, discrimination is still very real, just less obvious. You can see it in hiring decisions, promotions, team dynamics, or the assumptions people make about others based on race, gender, religion, or background.

When discrimination does show up—whether it's a direct comment, a clear pattern of unequal treatment, or a deeper systemic issue—it needs to be addressed head-on and openly. Ignoring it or brushing it aside sends the message that it's okay, which can destroy trust, morale, and the inclusive culture every organization should be aiming for.

Addressing bias and discrimination head-on isn't just about calling out the individuals involved. It's also about digging into the systems and patterns that allowed the behavior to happen in the first place.

Leaders need to take a strong, clear stand, showing that prejudice has no place in their organization. That might mean reevaluating hiring practices, offering diversity training, or even restructuring teams to make sure fairness and equity are built into the process.

But it's not enough to be reactive—leaders have to be proactive too. Discrimination isn't always obvious; it can hide in unconscious biases or long-standing workplace habits. A good leader looks at their own assumptions, has honest conversations with their team, and works to build a culture where diversity and inclusion are more than just goals—they're everyday realities.

Taking a firm stance on bias isn't just about protecting people or meeting compliance standards. It's about creating a workplace where everyone feels empowered to thrive, collaborate, and contribute their best.

By embracing diversity, organizations not only do what's right but also unlock the incredible power of different perspectives and experiences, driving innovation and long-term success.

The VP I mentioned earlier in the chapter—the one hiring only people who shared his faith—was a clear example of how bias can create a divided culture and hurt the entire company. I addressed the issue with him directly, making it clear how his actions were affecting not just his team but the organization as a whole.

Unfortunately, he refused to change. In the end, I had to transfer him to a less visible role with no staff under his supervision. It wasn't an easy or private decision, but it was necessary to protect the company's integrity and commitment to inclusivity.

Rigid thinking and biases can hold organizations back. To succeed, leaders need to stay open to fresh ideas, different perspectives, and approaches that challenge the way things have always been done. That's how you unlock the full potential of your team and stay ahead in a constantly changing world.

Here's another type of prejudice that's less obvious but just as harmful: the mindset of *"that's how we've always done it"* or *"we tried that three years ago, and it didn't work."* In a turnaround situation especially, this kind of thinking has to go. If it had worked so well in the past, you wouldn't be facing the challenges you are now. At the same time, dismissing an idea outright just because it didn't work before can shut down progress.

The fast pace of business often brings new opportunities for old ideas to succeed in fresh ways. Leaders need to create an environment where ideas aren't chance down too quickly but are given a fair chance until proven otherwise. Whether it's how you launch a product, communicate with customers, or structure responsibilities, everything needs to be reevaluated without bias, especially during times of change.

The mindset of *"I've seen it all before"* is another dangerous trap, often coming from past success. When someone solves a problem once, there's a tendency to assume the same approach will work for every new challenge. But every situation is different, and sticking to old strategies without adapting to the moment can hold you back.

Drawing on past experience is smart, but leaning too heavily on what worked before can lead to stagnation. Every situation is different, and strategies need to be adapted to fit the current context.

There are plenty of examples of successful leaders thriving in one industry but struggling when they move to another because they stick to the same old strategies.

Take Ron Johnson, for instance—he revolutionized retail at Apple but was unsuccessful at J.C. Penney by alienating its discount-focused customers. Similarly, Bob Nardelli's cost-cutting, numbers-driven approach from GE didn't mesh with Home Depot's customer-service–oriented culture. And John Sculley, who made waves at PepsiCo, couldn't translate those consumer goods strategies to Apple's fast-paced tech world.

Even after decades in consumer products, I've learned not to let past successes or instincts dictate decisions.

For example, when reviewing an advertising campaign, I know what worked before may not work again. Staying open to fresh ideas and adapting to the moment is what keeps me—and the organizations I've led—moving forward.

At this stage in my career, I recognize that I'm not always in tune with what motivates younger demographics or the cultural nuances of different markets. Every audience has its own values, attitudes, and ways of discovering products. To stay effective, I rely on people with fresh perspectives—those who can spot opportunities I might miss. It's a daily reminder to avoid the trap of assuming I already know what will work.

Speaking of assumptions, let's talk about another type of bias that stifles innovation: prejudice about job functions. For example, engineers don't know anything about marketing, right? They're all about numbers and data, so they can't possibly thrive in roles that require creativity or emotional intelligence. And of course, engineers and marketers can't communicate effectively, right?

Wrong.

These assumptions are not only inaccurate, but they're harmful to an organization's growth and potential. Why not challenge them? Put an engineer in the marketing department and see what happens. Chances are, the skills and perspectives they bring could lead to fresh ideas and solutions neither group would have discovered on its own. Breaking down these biases can unlock innovation and move the organization forward.

As a leader, it's on you to challenge these biases, both your own and those of your team.

Build a diverse group of individuals and create a culture where every voice, skill set, and perspective is genuinely valued. When you do, you're not just avoiding the pitfalls of bias; you're building an environment where your team can truly thrive and reach its full potential.

It's a truth that plays out even in the Marvel universe, perhaps nowhere more powerfully than in the story of Black Panther.

When we first meet T'Challa, King of Wakanda, he inherits more than a title, he inherits generations of isolationism and a deeply held belief that Wakanda's safety depends on keeping its advanced technology and knowledge hidden from the world. At first, he embraces this tradition, protecting his borders and preserving the status quo.

But after facing the fallout of past mistakes, including his father's choices and the rise of Killmonger, T'Challa begins to see things differently. He realizes that strength doesn't come from hiding behind walls, but from embracing connection, collaboration, and global responsibility. By the end of the film, he chooses to share Wakanda's resources, technology, and leadership with the world, rejecting prejudice and isolation in favor of inclusion and shared progress.

That evolution mirrors what great leaders must do: recognize when inherited assumptions or biases about people, ideas, or traditions, are holding back growth, and have the courage to change course. T'Challa's greatest strength wasn't his suit or his skills in combat; it was his willingness to listen, evolve, and bring others into the circle of influence.

That's what happens when you reject prejudice and embrace diversity, not just in race or culture, but in thought, background, and role. You build something stronger, more innovative, and far more prepared to face whatever's next.

Because once you start listening to every voice, not just the loudest or most familiar, you begin to see what real leadership can unlock.

DON'T BE SELF-IMPORTANT,
BE ACCESSIBLE

Modern business hierarchy in the US has always balanced structure with adaptability, shaped by historical shifts and cultural influences. When it's done right, that is.

After World War II, many companies adopted a military-like hierarchy, as returning veterans who had led troops to victory brought their command-and-control leadership styles into corporate America.

Leaders like Robert McNamara (captain, US Army Air Forces) at Ford, Henry Singleton (lieutenant, US Navy) at Teledyne, and Ernest Arbuckle (lieutenant commander, US Navy) at Wells Fargo epitomized this shift, applying the military's clear chains of command, disciplined execution, and results-driven strategies to business.

It made perfect sense at the time. The structured, no-nonsense approach that had worked in wartime translated seamlessly to the booming postwar economy, where efficiency and accountability were paramount. As McNamara put it, "The true measure of a manager is performance," a mindset that reflected the era's emphasis on achieving clear objectives and maintaining order in rapidly growing industries.

The military's influence on American business is a fascinating piece of history. It shows how strategies from one arena—war— can shape another—commerce—while highlighting the need for businesses to evolve as the world around them changes.

In the post–World War II business model, everything revolved around rank. Your title—manager, director, vice president, president, or chairman—wasn't just a designation; it dictated your entire corporate experience. The size of your office, where you parked, your travel budget, even how much respect you commanded in the boardroom—it all hinged on your spot in the hierarchy.

This rigid system also shaped the dynamics of leadership. Meeting your immediate supervisor was like an audience with the Pope. He (and yes, it was almost always a "he") sat behind an enormous desk, exuding authority, while you slumped in your chair, grateful just to be in his presence. The corporate ladder was a formal, clear-cut path to success, and breaking ranks was unthinkable.

And for a time, this model worked spectacularly. American companies thrived. The US economy was the undisputed global leader, bolstered by the fact that much of the world's industrial base lay in ruins.

While Japan and Europe were rebuilding from the ground up, the US churned out products and dominated global markets. In 1950, the US accounted for over 40 percent of global GDP—a testament to its economic might.

Companies embraced five-year plans and stuck to them religiously. Change wasn't just rare; it was practically nonexistent. This predictability seemed like a winning formula, and for a while, it was. Businesses operated like well-oiled machines, efficiently delivering results in a world with minimal competition.

This structure was ideal for industries like manufacturing, where precision and efficiency were key. Think assembly lines at General Motors or Ford. Everyone had a specific task, every part worked together, and the results were remarkable.

By the 1950s and 1960s, industrial giants like Chrysler, IBM, and Boeing dominated corporate America, driving the postwar economic boom. Studies show that between 1947 and 1973, the US economy grew at an impressive 4 percent annually, in large part because of these streamlined, structured corporate frameworks.

But this rigid approach had its drawbacks. While it worked brilliantly in predictable environments, it often stifled creativity and innovation. As industries evolved and markets became more dynamic, businesses realized they needed to change.

By the late twentieth century, companies began flattening their structures, cutting layers of management, and emphasizing collaboration—especially in tech and service industries, where agility mattered more than rigid control.

But things began to shift in the 1970s. Japan, once a struggling postwar economy, emerged as a formidable competitor. Their businesses were outperforming US companies, especially in industries like automobiles and electronics. By 1980, Japanese automakers like Toyota and Honda had captured a significant share of the US market, forcing American giants like Ford and General Motors to rethink their strategies.

The secret to Japan's success? A radically different corporate culture. Instead of rigid hierarchies, Japanese companies emphasized long-term planning, continuous improvement (kaizen), and consensus-driven decision-making.

Employees at all levels were encouraged to contribute ideas, and leadership prioritized teamwork over authoritarianism. The results were stunning: higher-quality products, greater efficiency, and a global reputation for innovation.

US businesses had no choice but to adapt. Companies began flattening hierarchies, embracing concepts like total quality management (TQM) and lean manufacturing—methods inspired by Japanese practices. For example, Ford implemented quality circles—small groups of employees who regularly met to identify and solve workplace issues—in the 1980s, directly borrowing from Toyota's playbook, and saw a noticeable improvement in production efficiency.

This shift marked the beginning of a cultural transformation in American business. The rigid, rank-obsessed model of the post–World War II era gave way to a more collaborative, flexible approach. While the old system had its successes, the wake-up call from Japan was a reminder that staying rigid in a dynamic world is the fastest way to fall behind.

Herb Kelleher, co-founder and former CEO of Southwest Airlines, exemplified accessible leadership. Unlike distant corporate executives, Kelleher stayed connected with employees at every level.

A standout example was when he loaded luggage with baggage handlers during the holiday rush—not for publicity, but to show no one, not even the CEO, was above pitching in. He also penned thousands of handwritten notes thanking employees for their hard work and celebrating their milestones, fostering loyalty and camaraderie.

Kelleher's humility and accessibility shaped Southwest's legendary customer service and operational success. As he put it, "It's not the planes that make Southwest successful. It's the people." His leadership proved that serving and empowering your team is far more impactful than maintaining a sense of superiority.

Herb Kelleher's humility made him a leader people wanted to follow, and I was about to learn my own lesson in staying grounded during one of my most unforgettable early experiences at Marvel: my first Comic-Con. This annual convention is like the Super Bowl for comic fans, and my first true public test as Marvel's head honcho.

This was about two months into my role as CEO, and I was still finding my footing. I was there with Stan Lee, the legendary co-creator of Marvel superheroes like Spider-Man and the Avengers, having just negotiated the contract that included his iconic cameos in Marvel movies. That day, I was Stan's wingman, plain and simple. He was the star, and I was there to keep up.

We walked into the main hall, shoulder to shoulder with the crowd, and it was like watching Moses part the Red Sea. Wherever

Stan went, people stepped aside, faces lighting up as they realized who was in their presence. Despite the overwhelming attention, Stan made himself approachable, stopping to chat with fans as if he had all the time in the world. As he paused to talk to someone, naturally, a crowd began to form around us.

Standing off to the side, I overheard a father and son nearby. The dad nudged his son, wide-eyed, and said, "John, that's Stan Lee!" You could hear the awe in his voice. The son, probably trying to make sense of the scene, asked, "Dad, who's the other guy?" Without missing a beat, the dad replied, "That guy? He's nobody."

In that moment, I got my comeuppance—two months into the job, and I was already being put in my place. It was a humbling reminder that no matter your title or position, the world doesn't revolve around you. And honestly, that's not a bad lesson to learn, especially as a leader.

That humbling moment at Comic-Con served as a powerful reminder that leadership isn't about basking in authority—it's about staying grounded, approachable, and adaptable, qualities that are essential in today's fast-changing business landscape. I also took solace in the fact that in the superhero industry, practically *everyone* is a nobody when they're standing next to Stan Lee!

Today's global economy is far too complex for the old-fashioned pyramid of power and authority to thrive. Flexibility and openness in strategy and thinking are critical to staying competitive, even for companies that maintain strong organizational structures. The pace of change in markets, technology, and customer preferences makes it impossible for rigid hierarchies to keep up.

Take the classic five-year plan—it's practically obsolete. As former General Electric CEO Jack Welch famously said, "Strategy is not a lengthy action plan. It is the evolution of a central idea through continually changing circumstances."

Within three months of drafting a plan, shifts in competition, tactics, or technology often render it outdated. Companies need leaders who can adapt quickly and guide their teams through constant change, often through a more collaborative structure that empowers employees to contribute ideas and adapt in real time.

The best leaders today don't lock themselves away in executive offices—they engage directly with their teams by walking around and fostering openness. Meetings, when held, are timely and informal, sparking real discussions rather than reinforcing hierarchy. Executives like Richard Branson of Virgin Group epitomize this approach: "I have an open-door policy. No matter how grand your title, you have to be willing to listen to everyone."

But there's a critical balance to strike. Interacting with employees is vital, but it must be done carefully. Giving direct instructions to employees several layers down the hierarchy can create chaos and resentment with their immediate supervisors. That's why I follow a simple rule: listen, don't direct.

For example, as chairman of the board for a company, I saw how quickly confusion could arise. A new board member, unfamiliar with corporate protocols, began giving instructions directly to employees. His intentions were good, but the fallout was immediate—resentment, unclear priorities, and a disrupted chain of command. I had to sit him down and explain that board members and senior leaders must never bypass managers.

Most experienced leaders understand this instinctively, but for newcomers, setting expectations is crucial. I always remind them: "You're welcome to talk to anyone, but never give direct instructions. That's not our role, and it undermines the leadership structure."

Leadership is about fostering trust and clarity, not micromanaging. Respecting the chain of command ensures smooth operations and strong relationships, creating a workplace where everyone knows their role and feels empowered to contribute. As Jeff Bezos of Amazon put it: "Leaders have to listen. Leaders also have to create an environment in which people are comfortable sharing their ideas." This kind of accessibility isn't just good optics—it's essential for fostering innovation and keeping an organization nimble.

Modern business also demands real-time awareness. Successful executives have structures in place to stay constantly updated on the state of their business, enabling them to react to threats almost overnight.

Leaders need their teams to feel comfortable bringing them information and ideas. Trust me when I say the days of rigid, top-down decision-making are over. Instead, the best executives foster stimulating exchanges with their teams, creating a collaborative environment where everyone feels empowered to contribute.

As legendary management consultant Peter Drucker put it, "The most important thing in communication is hearing what isn't said." A leader's openness and approachability aren't just about receiving information—they're about creating an atmosphere where employees feel their insights matter and their voices will be heard. That's how innovation happens, and that's how companies stay ahead in today's relentless competitive landscape.

LEARN FROM PAST PROBLEMS, BUT DON'T DWELL ON THEM

Mary Barra, Chair and CEO of General Motors, once poignantly remarked, "Looking at the road ahead through the rearview mirror will cause you to crash." This vivid analogy warns of the perils inherent in dwelling excessively on a company's past. When a new CEO assumes the mantle of leadership with the objective of steering a company toward new horizons, the tendency to fixate on past missteps can be a significant obstacle. In other words, it's a recipe to become a supervillain instead of a superhero leader.

This philosophy resonates deeply with my own approach to leadership and managing company turnarounds. Embracing Barra's insight, 95 percent of my time I'm focused on the present and the future, and only 5 percent of my time do I spend thinking about the past. It's crucial to learn from past failures but not be paralyzed by them, transforming these lessons into stepping stones toward greater achievements.

In practice, this approach means cultivating a forward-thinking culture where innovation and creative solutions are at the forefront, with a proactive mindset that seeks opportunities to excel and improve rather than dwelling on past errors. This focus on future potential allows us to drive the company toward a dynamic and successful trajectory.

It's important not to completely disregard the past, especially in a turnaround situation. Understanding the errors that brought the company to its current state is essential. Yet, the real challenge as a leader lies in balancing this awareness with a vision for the future. It's about acknowledging and learning from mistakes while ensuring they don't dominate our focus or sap our energy. By maintaining this balance, we keep the company moving forward, breaking free from destructive cycles and embracing new opportunities for growth and success.

Let me share an example from a time when I was brought in to lead an established but flailing organization. I decided to shake things up with the executive team, so I made a request that opened everyone's eyes. I asked each executive to jot down and share a list of their own slip-ups that they thought had contributed to the company's troubles. I also asked them what they would do going forward if they held my position. The looks on their faces? They were totally shocked by my request.

The responses I received were a fascinating glimpse into human behavior. Some executives were incredibly open, candidly sharing where they felt they had gone wrong. Others balanced their lists with not just their errors but also their successes, which provided a fuller picture of their impact on the company. However, a few came back to me insisting they couldn't think of any mistakes they'd made, quickly highlighting the shortcomings of others instead of admitting any of their own, and offering very little or no vision for the future.

It was a revealing moment that clearly identified who among us were excuse-makers and complainers. Needless to say, those individuals didn't last much longer at the company.

This experience wasn't just about identifying problems; it was about fostering a culture of accountability and self-reflection. Understanding failures and admitting them is a key step in moving past them—and hopefully avoiding them in the future. In leadership, it's crucial to encourage this kind of honesty and self-assessment, as it not only helps in understanding past failures but also paves the way for genuine growth and improvement.

When I step into a company teetering on complete failure, my focus isn't on the mistakes that got them here. Dwelling on past errors and pointing fingers isn't just unproductive; it also distracts us from the real work of rebuilding and moving forward. Honestly, there's just no time to waste on blame when there's so much positive work to be done.

Yet, it's inevitable that some folks will get stuck on what went wrong. They fixate on the negative, and frankly, that mindset can really drag down the morale and momentum of everyone else. Part of my job as a leader is to identify these downers early on—bringing them into the light so they can either adjust their attitude or move on.

This might sound harsh, but it's necessary. It sends a clear message to the rest of the team that looking backward and playing the blame game won't be tolerated. This approach really does help elevate the overall attitude and focus everyone on the future.

In any turnaround situation, you're managing a team of people that need to work their way out of the hole. Dealing with the team dynamics involves navigating between different personality types: the pessimists, the conservatives, and the optimists. Pessimists see every problem as a mountain too high to climb, and conservatives proceed with caution. And optimists? They view every challenge as an opportunity. My strategy isn't about turning everyone into an optimist overnight but about finding a balance. Once the pessimists are out of the picture, the conservatives and the optimists can really complement each other, creating a more balanced and healthier organizational environment.

Now, I'm not one to sugarcoat problems by calling them "opportunities." To me, that feels like a buzzword that doesn't help anyone. Problems are problems—plain and simple. But what I do find thrilling is solving these problems, pushing the business forward against the odds. In a turnaround situation, making tough decisions swiftly is crucial.

This might mean having to close manufacturing facilities, lay off staff, and cut back on benefits—unpleasant tasks that I liken to ripping off a Band-Aid. It's better to get these painful but necessary actions over with quickly, so we can start the healing process and rebuild on a solid foundation.

This approach isn't just about being tough; it's about being fair and clear, setting the stage for recovery, and ensuring the future success of the business.

When you're tasked with turning a company around, the reality is you can't fix everything on day one. It's just not feasible. But what you can do, and honestly need to do, is tackle the toughest, most painful decisions right off the bat. Getting those big, negative changes out of the way early sets the stage for recovery.

It's about clearing out the old baggage so you can start fresh. Think of it as setting a broken bone: the sooner you do it, the sooner healing can begin, and the sooner the company can start to find its new path. If you don't set a bone quickly, it's probably going to heal crookedly, and the same is true in business, if the organization doesn't go bankrupt first!

Once you've made the hard decisions, the key is to keep moving forward. Dwelling on past actions can stall progress. As C. S. Lewis said, "You can't go back and change the beginning, but you can start where you are and change the ending." Build on the changes you've initiated. That doesn't mean ignoring past lessons—but don't let them weigh you down.

I recall a meeting where we were discussing a new promotional idea, and someone said, "We tried that five years ago—it didn't work." At the time, we'd run a Father's Day promotion with Walmart, but it failed because their distribution system couldn't get the displays into stores. Fast-forward five years—Walmart had expanded rapidly and now had regional warehouses and better logistics. I encouraged the team to take a fresh look. We moved forward with the promotion—and it was a success.

That experience reinforced the point: conditions change. Don't dismiss a good idea just because it failed once. Keep looking ahead, stay adaptable, and act with confidence.

As leaders, we have to learn from the past, but we can't live in it. Whether it's a failed product launch, a toxic culture, or a painful restructuring, the job is to confront it, understand it, and then move forward, eyes on the road ahead.

Because progress doesn't come from rewriting the past.

It comes from choosing what to do next.

ESSENTIAL #8

ALWAYS (TRY TO) HIRE WORLD-CLASS PEOPLE

In my extensive career at the helm of various turnarounds, I've consistently found that the key to successful business recovery lies not just in strategies, but in the people who execute them.

These are not ordinary individuals; they are the brave souls who look at a failing enterprise and see a canvas of possibility. It's as crucial to convince talented people to stay with a turnaround company as it is to persuade new top-tier professionals to leave the security of a successful organization for a venture teetering on the brink. Both require a particular blend of audacity and persuasion. Turnarounds are indeed daunting—they demand a disposition that thrives on risk and sees opportunity where others see despair.

As the leader of such ventures, a sizable portion of my time was devoted to identifying, recruiting, and motivating these unique individuals. These are people who are invigorated by the challenges of a distressed business rather than deterred by them. They are comfortable navigating the uncertainty that turnarounds inevitably bring.

Most crucially, they placed their trust in me to guide them through the storm. Financial constraints often meant that I could not offer competitive salaries initially. Instead, my propositions were built on the potential for substantial stock options, the opportunity for profound professional growth, and a level of freedom rare in more stable environments. These candidates must believe in the vision and trust that their commitment will yield significant rewards.

Traditional executive search firms may not be suited to finding this type of talent. Firstly, the financial cost of employing such firms is usually prohibitive for a company in distress. Secondly, these firms typically lack the specialized research needed to identify individuals who excel in turnaround situations and have a proven track record.

My skepticism toward relying on search firms was cemented by an incident where I was asked to provide a reference for a former colleague. Despite my candid feedback to the search firm about his inadequate leadership and the damage he had caused our company, including a significant sexual harassment settlement, he was nevertheless hired for a top position in another company. He lasted only two years before his poor leadership brought that company to the brink of bankruptcy.

This experience underscored the importance of a more direct, personal approach in building a turnaround team. It's imperative to meticulously vet and personally engage potential team members, ensuring they not only possess the necessary skills but are also committed to the vision of revitalizing the company.

This hands-on recruitment strategy is crucial to assembling a group that is equipped and ready to navigate the turbulent waters of a turnaround and steer the company back to profitability.

I prefer to gather my own references, ideally through direct conversations—either in person or over the phone. Written recommendations, while useful, offer the recommender the opportunity to carefully edit and possibly sanitize their views.

In contrast, verbal references allow me to listen for nuances in tone, inflections, and observe body language if in person. These subtleties can reveal genuine confidence or hidden reservations about the candidate's suitability.

This meticulous approach to vetting candidates is time-consuming and often contrasts with the pressing urgency to fill critical positions in a struggling company.

However, the high-stakes nature of turnarounds leaves little room for error. The cost of bringing on the wrong person can be exceedingly high—far outweighing the temporary challenge of an unfilled position. It is far preferable to wait for the right candidate than to compromise and risk exacerbating the company's difficulties.

That said, there are certain situations when, in the interest of time, it's necessary to fill a position with someone who may not be world-class, but competent.

During my time as the leader of a number of hardware and construction product companies based in Italy, Germany, and the Netherlands. I faced the complex task of acquiring and integrating various other companies from around the globe into a unified operation. Each entity operated under a different business model, despite producing similar products.

This lack of synergy posed significant challenges, particularly when it came to streamlining operations and scaling back certain aspects of the companies. The success of such an initiative hinged not just on my leadership but critically on the caliber of the team I assembled. The process required leaders who could not only adapt to diverse business environments but also drive change sensitively and effectively.

Every step of building this team was guided by thorough vetting and the strategic patience to hold out for the right fit—principles I've adhered to throughout my career. Whether it's a high-stakes turnaround or a strategic reorganization, the foundational strategy remains the same: invest the time to find and recruit the right people, for they are the true architects of transformation.

This method has not only guided me through numerous professional challenges but has also reinforced the importance of trust and meticulousness in leadership decision-making.

Navigating the complexities of business operations in Europe presented unique challenges due to the stringent labor laws that govern workforce management. These laws often stipulated a thirty-two-hour work week, mandated five weeks of vacation annually, and nearly guaranteed perpetual employment, making any attempt to reduce the workforce an uphill battle.

In my case, the pressing need to cut back on labor costs at a factory not operating at full capacity was compounded by cultural perceptions. As an American executive from California, proposing efficiency improvements and workforce reductions, I was initially perceived negatively—seen as the stereotypical "ugly American" who failed to appreciate the quality of European manufacturing and the intricacies of its work culture.

Understanding that it was impractical and potentially ineffective to manage these changes remotely from an office in California, I recognized the need for a local intermediary who could bridge the cultural and operational divides.

Throughout my career, I have always prioritized finding individuals who not only possess high intelligence but also excel in people skills and intuitive understanding—traits essential for navigating complex and sensitive situations.

In this particular instance, my search was successful. I found a young, highly motivated national who had earned his MBA at Harvard Business School in the United States. His blend of American business acumen and deep understanding of the cultural norms made him an ideal candidate to advance our objectives locally.

This individual was not only intellectually equipped but also displayed remarkable resilience and a willingness to face unpopularity within his own community to achieve necessary outcomes. His efforts were pivotal; he persistently negotiated with the unions, overcame resistance from factory staff, and even secured cooperation from the government.

After more than six months of diligent effort, he successfully aligned the factory's workforce with its productivity needs, making the necessary adjustments to headcount without causing the upheaval that a more abrupt approach might have triggered. This experience underscored a critical lesson: the right person in the right role not only simplifies the leadership process but can also transform potentially volatile situations into opportunities for successful change.

Had I opted to impulsively close the factory or enforce layoffs without navigating the local labor landscape and securing governmental collaboration, the consequences would have been dire. This strategic placement and management approach proved once again that understanding and integrating into the local culture is not just a courtesy—it's a strategic imperative.

Recruiting quality talent to execute a vision is a task that requires serious consideration and strategic foresight. As a leader, it is imperative not only to evaluate the internal workforce but also to scrutinize the external professionals—ranging from auditors to legal advisors to advertising agencies—who are brought on to support the organization.

The standard for these roles must be set exceptionally high, sending a clear message to the industry and stakeholders that only the best is acceptable. This approach is not just about filling positions; it's about making a statement, rebuilding a company's reputation, and laying the groundwork for a successful recovery.

Moreover, effective governance is crucial and often hinges on the composition and engagement of the board of directors or management committee. One of the pervasive issues in American corporate culture is the selection of board members based on nepotism, reciprocal favors, or the allure of a powerful name rather than merit and expertise.

These practices lead to boards that are more focused on the perks of the position rather than the welfare of the company. Too often, board meetings can become perfunctory gatherings where members briefly discuss business matters before enjoying rich meals at the company's expense.

This scenario is far from what genuine guidance and leadership look like. Boards need to consist of individuals who possess relevant, actionable knowledge and who are committed to actively participating in the company's development frequently—ideally, on a weekly, and even at times, a daily basis.

When I took over at Marvel Entertainment in 1999, the board's composition reflected a range of interests, including those of some investors primarily focused on quick financial returns. This perspective was fundamentally at odds with a strategic vision of fostering long-term growth through sustainable business practices.

However, we also had a number of like-minded individuals on the board: turnaround specialists, just like me. To align the company's direction with its current capabilities, we adopted a licensing business model. This strategy leveraged Marvel's rich intellectual property—its comic book heroes—allowing the company to capitalize on its brands without incurring significant production costs.

Given Marvel's financial status at the time, having emerged from bankruptcy with limited assets other than its intellectual property, this model was more a necessity than a stroke of brilliance.

However, the success of a licensing model does not come overnight. It requires time not only to set up agreements but also to rebuild trust with partners who might have been burned by the company's previous financial collapse.

Reestablishing these relationships and convincing stakeholders to invest in a bankrupt entity again demands patience, a clear strategy, and a commitment to long-term results rather than immediate gains.

The initial reluctance from a few board members concerning our strategic shift was palpable, but ultimately, the substantial profits that materialized from our licensing model helped to alleviate their concerns.

Over time, we methodically began to phase out board members who were predominantly focused on short-term gains. In their place, we appointed individuals who shared a vision for cultivating a robust and enduring business framework at Marvel.

Having board members who are not only present but deeply engaged in our daily operations was crucial to the execution of our strategic goals. At Marvel, board involvement went well beyond the customary quarterly meetings. Our board members were integral to our operations, contributing weekly to our strategic discussions without micromanaging the finer details of day-to-day execution.

In my opinion, we had an all-star board after one year.

Marvel's board achieved notable success, a testament to the deep-rooted commitments each member upheld regarding our business philosophies.

These principles included viewing guidance as an opportunity rather than a constraint, allowing business processes to unfold organically, prioritizing liquidity over mere profit figures, and focusing on long-term results rather than short-term gains. This approach is somewhat unusual for the boards of publicly traded companies, where the need to publicly report immediate financial returns often overshadow broader strategic goals.

To align the interests of our board members with the long-term health and success of the company, Marvel compensated its directors not just with a salary, but more significantly, with shares of Marvel stock. This pay-for-performance arrangement ensured that our board members were directly invested in the company's success, mirroring the incentives of other stakeholders.

Offering stock options as compensation is an effective strategy for attracting top-tier executive talent to a company in the midst of a turnaround, particularly when financial resources are constrained. This method not only made board positions more attractive but also more affordable for the company.

However, this approach is unconventional for two primary reasons. Firstly, it's possible for senior managers, especially CEOs, to feel threatened when highly accomplished board members are actively involved in coaching operations and interact regularly with senior management. Such a dynamic can be perceived as undermining their authority or diluting their influence within the company.

Secondly, this model of an "active board" requires a high level of confidence and self-assurance from all executives involved. They must prioritize the company's interests above their own professional egos, a necessity that demands significant personal maturity and a strong sense of corporate stewardship.

From my perspective, I prefer to bring on highly accomplished people early, when you can secure top-tier help at the most affordable rates. It may seem surprising, but many are willing to work for equity and modest board fees rather than full-time salaries. That's the bargain—you gain exceptional expertise without the cost of a full-time executive. Board members are a great example: for limited compensation, they bring strategic insight, credibility, and connections. They understand it's not a full-time role, but their impact—on the business and in attracting other top talent—can be significant. At Marvel, we believed that our distinctive approach to board involvement set us apart. It encouraged a transparent, inclusive, and dynamic governance culture that was exceptionally beneficial to the company. Further, the culture of our company, and especially that of our board, was built around the idea that we were going to change the rules of the game.

We decided not to compete in the industry like everyone else. The success of this model hinges on the mutual respect and trust between the board and management, facilitated by a shared commitment to the company's long-term vision.

This system, though demanding, proved to be a crucial factor in our sustained growth and industry leadership, reflecting a corporate ethos that valued strategic depth and collaborative leadership over hierarchical control.

Conventional wisdom frowns upon giving equity as payment with the claim that it offers temptation to board members to inflate stock prices. That is ridiculous. If, as a leader of a company, you are seriously worried about the character of your board members, then do not hire them.

If you inherited board members that are unscrupulous or self-interested, get rid of them. If your board, however, shows the commitment and investment of personal time and energy that Marvel' s had shown, they will be rewarded fairly by the success they helped create.

Here are three takeaways that you can implement in your professional life:

1. **Thorough Vetting Process:**
   - **Implementation**: Prioritize in-depth vetting for potential hires, especially for pivotal roles. Ensure thorough interviews, personal reference checks, and cultural fit assessments to avoid costly hiring mistakes.
2. **Strategic Compensation Planning:**
   - **Implementation**: Utilize inventive compensation strategies like substantial stock options or performance-based incentives to attract top talent, especially useful in resource-limited environments like startups or companies undergoing turnarounds.
3. **Cultivate a Trust-Based Culture:**
   - **Implementation**: Develop a corporate culture centered on transparency, mutual respect, and strategic alignment. Engage all levels of staff in regular strategic discussions to foster commitment and ensure everyone feels valued and aligned with the company's goals.

Looking back, the lesson is simple but powerful: world-class people make world-class outcomes possible. No strategy, no matter how clever, can succeed without the right people to bring it to life. In every turnaround I've led, the true engine of recovery wasn't me—it was the team I built. The people who believed in the mission, trusted the process, and gave everything they had when it mattered most.

It's a truth I touched on back in essential #4, and one worth revisiting here: Professor Charles Xavier didn't just lead with empathy, he hired with vision.

In the Marvel universe, Professor X is the rare kind of leader who builds an extraordinary team not by playing it safe, but by identifying untapped potential in people the world had written off. The X-Men weren't the obvious picks. Many had unpredictable powers. Some had checkered pasts. But Xavier didn't just look at who they were, he saw who they could become.

And he didn't hire for loyalty alone. He recruited for character, courage, and capacity. People like Storm, Cyclops, and Jean Grey weren't just powerful; they were aligned. They believed in the mission. That's what turned a group of outcasts into a force for global change.

Great hiring works the same way. You don't build a team of résumés; you build a team of belief. You find the people who see the challenge not as a red flag, but as a call to action. People who want in, not because it's easy, but because it matters.

Because when you hire world-class people, and give them a reason to believe, you don't just turn around a company.

You build something extraordinary.

FIND A FEW PEOPLE WHO WILL TELL YOU THE TRUTH, EVEN WHEN IT HURTS

Few characters in the Marvel universe are willing to stand up to Wolverine, *especially* once the claws have come out. But that's just what his allies Captain America and Storm do on a regular basis when the iconic hero is barking up the wrong tree. Being a leader isn't too different!

Much like how Captain America and Storm challenge Wolverine, in leadership, it's crucial to have people who aren't afraid to stand up and tell you the hard truths. It's easy to surround yourself with yes people who will flatter you and tell you everything's going fine when, deep down, you know there's work to be done. But finding those people who will challenge you—who will stand up and say, "Hey, you missed the mark here" or "I don't agree with that"—is how you grow. It's how you get better.

When I first step into a new role, whether at a new company or in a new industry, it feels like learning a new language. Everything is different: the terms, the expectations, even the culture. It is like walking into a foreign land where every word and action carry a different meaning. At times, it's overwhelming. But I knew one thing for sure: I needed the truth. I can still remember my first few weeks at one of my early jobs. You know, the kind of position where you want to make a great first impression but are also concerned about messing things up? My mind was filled with questions like: How do I identify the right people? How do I know who I can trust to give me honest feedback? And how do I create an environment where those people aren't afraid to speak their minds?

Well, it didn't happen overnight, but I learned to actively seek out individuals who had the courage to speak the truth, even when it wasn't easy. These people became my mentors. Some were people I had known from past roles; others were new faces.

But regardless of their background, they shared one critical trait: a very strong interest in improving the business. They didn't just want to be people eagerly nodding "yes" to every new idea—they wanted to make things better. That was the key. They were willing to tell me what needed to be said, no matter how uncomfortable it might have been.

And this goes back to something I shared with you in essential #4, about a small group of my reports at Bristol-Meyers who made me painfully aware that I didn't appear to be listening to them when it came to making decisions. It was a tough lesson to learn, but one I'm grateful for.

I had been making choices and implementing plans without seeking enough input from the team. The result? A disconnect. A sense that I wasn't listening, even though I thought I was. They weren't afraid to speak directly, and I'll never forget the discomfort that came with hearing their feedback. It wasn't easy to admit, but it was necessary. They showed me that I needed to slow down and listen more, because my decisions weren't just mine—they affected the whole team.

I distinctly remember reaching out to one of my mentors after landing a new position at a company. There was a situation that was out of my depth, and I needed guidance. I said, "Hey, I'm here now, and I'm trying to figure this out. Can you help me think through this?" And you know what he said? "Sure. But first, tell me what you think. What's your take?" I loved that about him. Instead of giving me a quick answer, he pushed me to think for myself, to dig deeper into the problem.

The same goes for the people I worked with. I made it clear that I valued honesty. I would say things like, "I just want to get better. I'm not perfect, so if you see something I can improve, tell me. I need to hear it." Most on my team didn't take this at face value—they had worked for plenty of people that considered constructive criticism to be a fireable offense. But I proved I meant what I said.

It took a little courage for some people to open up, but over time, they learned I wasn't going to fire them or get mad at them for offering constructive feedback. Instead, I wanted them to tell me more. "Tell me why you think that. What should I have done differently? What can we change moving forward?"

It wasn't just subordinates who spoke up, either. I've had bosses who didn't hold back when they thought I was off track. I had one boss, in particular, who really stands out. After a particularly tough decision, he pulled me aside and said, "Peter, why did you go in that direction? What were you thinking?" At first, it stung. But the more I thought about it, the more I realized he was doing me a favor. He wasn't trying to tear me down—he wanted me to be better. He wanted me to think more critically and make better decisions moving forward.

That's when it clicked for me—this was the kind of feedback leaders needed. Not just from my team, but from my peers and even my superiors. I've been lucky in that sense. Having served under great bosses—both in the navy and in business—who weren't afraid to challenge me. They wanted me to succeed. They pushed me, and it was uncomfortable at times, but it was always worth it.

So how do you find these people? It's not always easy, and it certainly doesn't happen right away. But trust is key. Trust builds slowly over time, and once you've established that trust with someone, they're more likely to speak up when something's wrong.

You can't just hire people and expect them to start giving you honest feedback right off the bat. It takes time. It takes showing them that you genuinely care about their input, even when it's hard to hear.

Interestingly, I've never been able to pinpoint one single attribute in these truth-tellers. Some were optimists, others pessimists. Some were extroverted, others quiet and reserved. What they all had in common was a deep, unwavering commitment to improving the business. They cared about the outcome just as much as I did. They were willing to speak up because they knew it would make the company better in the long run.

One example comes to mind: we were strongly considering acquiring an established company in the beauty industry. The deal looked promising—it would have expanded our product line in a related category and improved our company's visibility on retail shelves. I was strongly in favor of moving forward. But before we pulled the trigger, I reached out to a few of my direct reports and asked, "What do you think we should do here?" I was genuinely curious to hear their thoughts.

One executive spoke up and said, "I don't think we should move forward with this. Here's why…" They explained that while the target company had a solid reputation, it was a traditional, slow-moving operation that didn't seem equipped to adapt to rapid changes, especially in an industry increasingly shaped by digital innovation.

At first, I didn't agree. I believed the deal had strategic value. But after really listening and considering their point of view, I realized they were right. We ultimately decided to walk away.

Just a month later, another company, one we didn't directly compete with, announced a breakthrough in beauty tech: a radically new way to deliver beauty products to consumers that completely leapfrogged the company we had considered acquiring. Their business was effectively disrupted overnight.

Looking back, had we gone through with the acquisition, we would have been saddled with a fading brand just as the market moved forward without it. That experience reaffirmed the importance of listening to, and trusting, the team around me. Truthfully, I would have done the deal. But this was a powerful reminder that not all risks are worth taking, and in this case, charging ahead would have been a costly mistake. I've always believed in making feedback a two-way street. The more someone shares with me, the more I want to share with them. I made it clear to my team that I wanted their thoughts—not just in passing, but in real time, so that we could adjust things on the fly if necessary.

Of course, I wasn't perfect in my feedback, but I always made sure to deliver it in a supportive way. I never took the critical, parental approach with my team. I was more like a supportive parent, guiding them and helping them improve without tearing them down.

As time went on, these conversations became a regular part of our interactions. It wasn't always formal feedback or critiques. Sometimes, it was just casual conversations that helped clarify things. And that kind of honesty paid off in a big way. It helped prevent issues, and more importantly, it often led to quick solutions that could have been overlooked if we hadn't been so open with each other.

One specific example that stands out took place early in my career at W.R. Grace. At the time, I was fresh out of Harvard, and I was still learning how to navigate the corporate world. The culture at Grace was deeply problematic, and I quickly realized that it was driven by people more interested in tearing others down to look good themselves than actually improving the business. It was the kind of toxic environment where the more you embarrassed someone, the more you were rewarded.

So, during one of the company's infamous financial reviews—where it felt more like gladiators in a Roman amphitheater than a corporate meeting—I asked a fairly straightforward question. I wasn't trying to be confrontational, but it clearly came across the wrong way. I asked a person running a big division a question about their operations, and they took offense. They were so defensive, likely because they were so used to getting criticized that they saw even a simple question as an attack. The whole thing left me feeling bad because, in my mind, I was just trying to understand and contribute.

It wasn't just the feedback that saved me; it was also the guidance from those who knew when to steer me away from making rash decisions. The senior advisor I mentioned earlier could see exactly what I was thinking when I was ready to confront the individual who had attacked me unfairly.

He could read me well, and his advice was exactly what I needed at the time. "Peter, don't do it," he said, sensing the storm brewing inside me. "I know how you're thinking. You'd be making a mistake. The guy who looks bad right now is the one who attacked you for no reason. You don't need to reciprocate. Stay above this."

I paused, taking in what he said. At first, it didn't register immediately. Why shouldn't I fight back? But he had seen the bigger picture. "It's not going to work well for you personally or for him," he continued. "You have to be unemotional. Ask another question, but keep it positive. Make it a layup—ask him something about his division, make him feel like you value his expertise."

"Like what?" I asked, still not completely sure.

"Ask him how his automotive aftermarket parts business is going. Its sales are up 15%. Act like you don't know, like you want to learn. Ask how he sees the future," Alex suggested. "You're going to turn this around, and it'll work in your favor."

It was a simple, yet genius move. I took his advice to heart. When I returned to the meeting, I didn't escalate things. I turned to the person who'd been defensive and asked, "How's your automotive aftermarket parts business going? How do you see the future for that segment?"

The change in tone was immediate. Instead of hostility, the person was suddenly on the defensive in a good way, forced to discuss his area of expertise. And guess what? We became friends. What could've been an ongoing battle turned into a productive conversation. The situation was defused, and the guy I had originally butted heads with ended up respecting me for how I handled it.

That was a turning point for me. Alex, who had been with the company much longer, saw the bigger picture. He understood that sometimes the best way to win wasn't to fight back but to rise above the situation, stay calm, and show you are the bigger person. That's something I carry with me in every leadership situation— keep it cool, collected, and, if necessary, ask the right questions to shift the energy in the room.

You might think that by letting the situation go, I was avoiding confrontation, but here's the thing: as a leader, sometimes you have to put your ego aside. It's not easy, especially when you feel wronged, but I've learned the biggest mistake you can make is letting your ego drive your decisions.

As a leader, you have to balance confidence with humility. You don't want to be so confident it turns into arrogance, nor so humble that people don't take you seriously. I've always tried to keep my ego in check. I never see myself as "better" than anyone else. Sure, I may have more experience or a different background, but I've always been comfortable with who I am. And when you're at ease with yourself, people respond positively.

Now, there's someone who's really been essential in keeping my ego in check, and that's my amazing wife, Maris. As of this writing, we've been married for fifty-four years, and let me tell you, she's seen it all. She's had to put up with a lot of my impatience, especially when I was focused on turnarounds. It's great for business, but not so great for family life. Maris had no problem calling me out when I was being difficult or letting my ego get the better of me.

Maris has always known how to keep me in check, especially after I'd return from long business trips. I'd march in, ready to shake things up and impose my "brilliant" ideas, only for Maris to remind me they did just fine without me.

And vacations? I used to get so caught up in not "wasting time" that I'd be on edge until about halfway through, when I'd finally start to relax. But just as I began to unwind, the thought of work piling up would have me wound up all over again. My grand-kids even started calling me "Grumpy Grandpa," which I couldn't stand—it wasn't that I was grumpy, really, just incredibly impatient. Maris never hesitated to call me out. She'd just look at me and say, "No, you're not doing that. Stop it, Peter." And you know what? Most of the time, I'd actually listen. She has this knack for cutting right through my impatience, reminding me to just be there, in the moment, with everyone.

And that's the thing about ego. Sometimes, it's not so obvious. You don't always recognize when it's creeping up. But people close to you, like Maris, can see it immediately. She reminds me to be present, let others talk, and, most importantly, not let my impatience affect those around me.

This reminds me of Founding Father John Adams and his relationship with his wife, Abigail. They exchanged letters almost daily while he was away. Abigail was his sounding board, offering encouragement or a tough push when needed.

In many ways, Maris has been my Abigail. She's my trusted partner, always there to ground me and offer perspective, whether I'm at my best or my worst.

Like Abigail, Maris knows when I need to hear the hard truths. She's called me out on my ego and reminded me when I'm being impatient or missing something important, especially during stressful times in my career. For that, I'm incredibly lucky.

This kind of partnership has been essential for me, both as a leader and as a person. Not everyone finds such a relationship, but it's been invaluable in helping me stay focused on what truly matters—building trust, making tough decisions, and finding balance in everything I do.

Looking back, I can honestly say that the people who told me the truth, even when it hurt, helped shape who I am as a leader. They made me better. They helped me grow. And I will forever be grateful for their honesty and their courage. Because at the end of the day, it's the truth-tellers who are the real superheroes in any organization.

CREATING A NEW CULTURE: A LEADER'S TOUGHEST JOB. THE WALTZ OR THE TANGO. WHICH STYLE IS APPROPRIATE?

Changing a company's culture is a leader's monumental challenge, second only to maintaining the emotional resilience required to make tough decisions that may not sit well with everyone.

At its core, organizational culture is about how we treat those we work with: our employees, business partners, customers, and investors. This treatment reflects not just how we operate; it's a mirror of our organization's personality and what we truly value in our interactions.

Moreover, a culture is also about setting priorities that will define success. What's paramount? Technology, customer service, or product innovation? While we aim to excel in all areas, recognizing which aspects to prioritize is vital. This prioritization doesn't just set our goals—it aligns our resources to excel where it matters most, guiding the strategic direction of our business and ensuring we dance to the right rhythm in the ever-evolving marketplace.

Understanding how to master the right corporate dance—whether leading with the grace of a waltz, the passion of a tango, or the flexibility of a cha-cha that falls somewhere in between—is crucial for effectively navigating the varied rhythms of business challenges.

Reflecting on my journey through various corporate turn-arounds, I've often found subtle parallels between my leadership style and the last thing you'd ever expect—my days as a disc jockey during my final year in college. Just as a DJ must read and adapt to the shifting dynamics of the audience, a leader must similarly gauge and shape the evolving culture of their organization, tuning into the feedback loops and rhythms of their team to orchestrate a cohesive and motivated workforce.

Yes, I wasn't always spinning companies away from failure; back in college, I would occasionally spin records at the campus radio station under the infamous moniker of "King Pleasure," a name I borrowed from a jazz musician at the time. I wasn't playing any jazz; I just thought it was a cool name.

It wasn't a formal, regular show but a spontaneous, fun activity where I'd just drop by the station whenever the mood struck me to play some records. I enjoyed experimenting with music and sometimes even channeled a famous Philadelphia disc jockey, Jocko Henderson and his Rocket Ship Show, introducing songs in rhymes just for fun. This experience unknowingly taught me about creativity and connecting with an audience. If any of my fans from those days happen to be reading this book, this next chapter is dedicated to you.

Though the broadcast radius of the station—and the actual time on the air—may have been limited, the lessons gained were invaluable. Learning how to read an audience and choosing the right song at just the right moment has not only been a skill in my DJ days but has also served me well in my professional life, teaching me the importance of timing and perception in leadership.

My passion for music extended beyond the DJ booth; it inspired me to bring the artists I played on air to perform live on campus, helping fund my college education. With my youthful audacity, I ventured to the heart of Manhattan's music scene, the iconic Brill Building on Broadway, a melting pot of musical creativity. Walking through the halls, echoing with the sounds of pianos clacking and singers rehearsing, it felt like traveling through the very heart of the music industry.

Walking through doors unannounced, I got the chance to chat directly with artists or their reps about performing at our Alfred. I actually managed to book big names like Wilson Pickett, along with other stars like Dionne Warwick and Little Anthony and the Imperials. It was a blast and really brought some excitement to campus.

The summer before my final year in college, I switched from the scholarly campus life to the exciting nightlife of West Greenwich Village, landing a job as a dancer at Trude Heller's—a classic '60s hotspot that was loud, hot, and sweaty. It was a place where icons like Cyndi Lauper, the Beastie Boys, and Manhattan Transfer would get their starts. Dancing in bell bottom pants on a platform, I was plunged myself into that classic '60s scene, meeting characters who were as memorable and eccentric as they come.

After graduating in 1967, I found myself working in a fiberglass factory in New Jersey across the river from Philadelphia, a city buzzing with soul music that rivaled Motown's hit-making machine. I remember Hy Lit, a renowned Philadelphia disc jockey, who hosted weekends at venues featuring local acts—occasionally, I joined his troupe as a dancer. These venues were more than just bars; they were large spaces that formed the heart of the Philadelphia Sound.

Reflecting on these experiences, it is clear that my journey has been as much about the vibrant, sometimes quirky paths I've navigated as the destinations themselves. Whether behind the mic or on the dance floor, each experience was a stepping stone in understanding leadership, culture, and engagement. These lessons in adaptability, reading the room, building relationships, fostering creativity, and maintaining purpose under pressure have been invaluable.

In my corporate roles, discerning whether a company's culture calls for the structured elegance of a waltz or the spirited passion of a tango has become essential. Much like a DJ gauges whether the audience wants timeless classics or the latest hits, I've needed to assess whether an organization is poised to seize new opportunities or requires a familiar tune to ease into change.

In more traditional settings, navigating a corporate turnaround is like following the steps of a waltz—everyone knows their role and what comes next, providing a sense of stability and predictability. Conversely, in creative dynamic industries like tech or design, leading is more like performing a tango, where spontaneity and creativity take the lead. Effectively managing these transformations involves knowing when to stick with the tried-and-true and when to innovate, always tuning your leadership to your team's needs.

This ability to "change the music" becomes crucial when transforming a company's culture, especially one lacking direction. Merely announcing a new direction isn't enough; leadership must be performed with consistency and authenticity, demonstrated through actions, not just words.

In creative environments like advertising, where innovation is crucial, the passionate tango fits perfectly. However, it's important to ensure this enthusiasm doesn't spiral out of control. Conversely, in conservative sectors like banking, the structured simplicity of the waltz is ideal, matching the precision and orderliness these fields demand.

This dance analogy highlights that every company has its unique rhythm and needs, underscoring the importance of a leader's ability to adapt their style for organizational success.

For example, a tech giant like Google operates vastly differently from a traditional healthcare company, not just in procedures but also in the types of people they employ and their fundamental values. Recognizing these distinctions is essential, particularly when stepping into a new role or during mergers and acquisitions, which often combine entities with completely different operational rhythms.

I've frequently seen companies where the allocation of resources doesn't align with their stated priorities. It's all too common for firms to declare their dedication to innovation while relegating their least capable staff to spearhead crucial projects. Such misalignment, typically a result of poor leadership, establishes a workplace atmosphere that employees pick up on, usually resulting in widespread underperformance.

This scenario was all too familiar when I joined Marvel post-bankruptcy. The company was like a patient recovering from intense chemotherapy: technically cured but having lost all its hair, much like Marvel had lost much of its top talent. Many of our best people had left, unwilling to wait for a resurgence, leaving behind a culture mired in uncertainty that was more about survival than growth.

Turning Marvel around required more than just smart business decisions; it demanded a complete overhaul of our operational ethos. We needed to reject the industry's wasteful habits in filmmaking and comic book production, building a lean and efficient culture ready for success. Our culture could best be described as "changing the rules of the game."

For this culture to succeed, support from key figures within the company was crucial. Our board, experienced in corporate turnarounds, provided unwavering support. Avi Arad, who spearheaded our move into the film industry, and Joe Quesada, our editor-in-chief, were instrumental in this transformation.

Joe revitalized our comic book line by bringing back top talent and infusing our stories with new energy. His desire for creative freedom led to the creation of Marvel Knights, an imprint that gave fresh takes on classic characters like Daredevil, Elektra, Black Widow, and others. This initiative, along with the Marvel Ultimates line that reimagined groups like the X-Men and the Hulk for new audiences, was pivotal in our strategy to appeal to both longstanding fans and new readers.

We simplified the Marvel universe for newcomers by updating origin stories, such as changing Spider-Man's powers from a bite by a radioactive spider to a bite from one that was genetically engineered. This approach made our stories more relevant and accessible.

Additionally, Bill Jemas, who I recruited from a major sports league, played a crucial role. Although not all the ideas were his, Bill was instrumental in advocating for bold, innovative strategies during our meetings, which transformed our team into a powerhouse of creativity and innovation.

And then there was Ike Perlmutter, our controlling shareholder, whose rigorous cost management and meticulous attention to detail were vital in reshaping our operational ethos. With the right team and the right mindset, we weren't just patching up Marvel; we were completely redefining the company's operational blueprint.

During my tenure, we not only produced highly successful movies that met our high standards but also pinpointed areas needing significant enhancement, particularly in licensing. For instance, we found that the quality of some merchandise produced by our licensees was low-quality or just average, which was clearly unacceptable.

To ensure our high standards were consistently met, we instituted strict quality control measures. We required physical samples of every licensed product to be examined before they were shipped to customers. This hands-on approach was crucial in rebuilding Marvel's reputation and ensuring that every aspect of our operations reflected the excellence we strived for.

Since I had no background in film or comic books, deepening my understanding of Marvel's universe was essential for aligning its culture with our operational needs—almost like choosing the right music for a dance. This effort included immersing myself in the monthly comic book issues to quickly get up to speed with the essence of each superhero, a step that proved indispensable for effective leadership.

However, the true credit for our creative success belongs to the outstanding team mentioned earlier. While I took the time to understand the Marvel universe, my primary role was to facilitate their best work by not interfering; I reviewed scripts but never made changes. My focus was on adhering to essential #8 of our guiding principles: always hire world-class talent. This strategy not only brought in high-quality individuals who consistently rose to the occasion but also emphasized the importance of trusting exceptional teams to deliver exceptional results.

I've learned that strategies effective in one context might not work in another. It's a common pitfall for leaders to cling to famil-iar approaches instead of adapting to new challenges, often letting ego overshadow the need for change.

I've seen many colleagues thrive in one setting only to falter in another, a vital lesson that past success doesn't always predict future results. Being open to learning, adapting, and sometimes starting anew is essential for any leader. At Marvel, this wasn't a problem because we had strong innovators at every level. For us, "changing the rules of the game" was a natural evolution, continuously driv-ing us toward innovative solutions and keeping us competitive.

This need for adaptability becomes clear when dealing with internal corporate dynamics, such as the often strained relation-ships between corporate staff and business unit leaders. These ten-sions can significantly influence decision-making processes. Early in my career at a conglomerate, it was apparent that a deep-seated distrust and even resentment existed between the operational teams and the corporate staff. This environment fostered a cul-ture where criticism was common, and recognition came only from pointing out flaws in others' plans—a dynamic I found quite disheartening.

Desperate to escape a toxic corporate atmosphere, I was deter-mined to find a role where I could make a positive impact on the business, not just offer critiques. After a challenging year, I managed to move into one of the business units.

However, the broader corporate culture remained deeply flawed and almost militaristic. Success was measured by "gotcha" moments—a toxic metric that hardly fostered a thriving environment. This was a corporate dance I couldn't perform, fundamentally misaligned with my values and vision for effective business practices.

This situation underscored a critical lesson: it's not just about needing to adapt or change your approach—it's about recognizing that some organizational cultures are simply not the right fit, no matter how hard you try. Just like a good dancer knows which steps they can pull off—good at the tango, weak at the waltz.

In a similar vein, when we were rebuilding Marvel after its bankruptcy, it wasn't enough just to bring back top talent; we needed a complete transformation of our approach. We had to revitalize our brand and inject our products with fresh, innovative ideas. This effort was about more than just financial recovery—it was about taking bold, calculated risks to completely redefine Marvel's identity.

But redefining a company's future isn't just about fixing operations—it's about reshaping how people think, act, and collaborate. At Marvel, we weren't just recovering; we were rewriting the rhythm of the entire organization—shifting from survival mode to a culture driven by innovation, purpose, and belief.

That's what cultural change demands. Not abandoning your principles, but learning to dance to a different rhythm. To move from the precision of a waltz to the improvisation of a tango. To lead in sync with the future, not the past.

Because creating a new culture isn't just about what the company *says*, it's about what the leader *shows*. And once the music changes, your job isn't to freeze. It's to move with purpose. To listen, adjust, and lead the next step.

NAVIGATING THE MAZE: BALANCE STRUCTURE WITH FLEXIBILITY

All organizations have a unique maze—a distinct way decisions get made and ideas move forward. Like a dance, the maze often reflects the industry it operates in. A good leader learns to navigate the maze and reach the desired outcome. Bad leaders can get lost forever, or worse yet meet the Minotaur in the middle of the labyrinth.

Take banks, for example. Their maze is typically highly structured and complex, designed to be thorough and risk-averse. Decisions take time, and that's intentional. Paperwork piles up to meet strict regulatory requirements, multiple executives weigh in, and those same executives often sit on overlapping committees. In a bank, this meticulous process makes sense. It's not a place for quick, impulsive moves—people's money and trust are at stake.

Now contrast that with an ad agency, where creativity and quick thinking rule the day. Here, the maze is simpler and far more flexible, offering multiple pathways to decision-making. Individuals are empowered to act because mistakes, when they happen, are easier to fix. Unlike a bank, an ad agency doesn't operate under heavy regulations or rigid formulas.

The focus is on innovation and originality, not compliance. A streamlined maze encourages employees to experiment, take risks, and think outside the box. By examining the maze, you can pinpoint where employees feel empowered to unleash their potential and avoid letting bureaucracy stifle creativity.

Now, imagine stepping into a company in crisis—a turnaround situation. You'll almost always find a maze that's completely out of sync with the business's needs. That's often a big reason why the company is struggling in the first place.

Turnaround mazes are oversized, unnecessarily complicated, and often designed in ways that actively block progress. The more innovative or radical an idea, the harder it becomes to move through the maze. Even in industries that thrive on flexibility and fresh thinking, these businesses create roadblocks that suffocate creativity and stall decision-making.

For instance, if every decision—no matter how small—requires sign-off from multiple vice presidents, you're looking at a maze built to inhibit progress. Instead of enabling action, the system gets bogged down by redundant layers of approval and outdated processes.

A CEO stepping into this kind of environment has a tough task ahead: dismantling a maze that thwarts decisiveness and rebuilding one that empowers employees to act and succeed. The maze isn't just about how decisions are made; it reflects the company's culture, priorities, and, ultimately, its path to survival.

In 1983, I became president of Clairol Appliances International. I encountered a maze where the walls weren't just figurative, they were international borders. The division operated across twenty-five countries, but most of the research, development, and manufacturing were centralized in the US.

At first glance, centralizing production seemed logical—it streamlined operations, or so we thought. But in practice, it created enormous challenges, especially as competition in our market intensified. Our mandate was clear: innovate or die. New products weren't just helpful; they were essential for survival, driving at least 30 percent of our revenue annually.

Sometimes innovation meant tweaking existing products—a small improvement, like adding a new button to a hairdryer, could make all the difference. Other times, it required creating entirely new product categories, like the then-revolutionary foot spas. But no matter the scope, success depended on seamless collaboration across borders—and that's exactly where the system broke down.

Years of inconsistent leadership had left the organization divided, with cultural differences largely overlooked. European branches openly distrusted their American counterparts. In some cases, the friction was so bad that European managers outright refused to communicate with US colleagues. They saw American-made products as low quality, unsuitable for their markets—and frankly, they weren't always wrong.

The disconnect between European customers' expectations and what was being produced in the US created an almost insurmountable roadblock. This mistrust wasn't just an internal nuisance; it was a fundamental threat to progress. How could we innovate and stay competitive when half the organization didn't even want to sell the other half's products?

Before we could push forward with new ideas, we had to bridge the cultural divide. Without trust and alignment, the maze of innovation would remain impassable, and our mandate to innovate would stall before it even began.

Adding to the complexity, each country in Clairol's portfolio had unique needs for its product lines, shaped by differing electrical standards, cultural preferences, and consumer habits. But the company's one-size-fits-all structure required every country to sell every product, regardless of fit.

Take the "Panic Button" Personal Protection Alarm, for instance. In the US, where personal security was a growing concern and car alarms were surging in popularity, the product made sense. But in Europe, where personal safety wasn't viewed the same way at the time, women didn't see the need. Clairol was offering a solution to a problem that didn't exist, and unsurprisingly, the product flopped overseas.

On the flip side, Clairol's Danish factory was producing top-quality hot rollers. While the product itself was exceptional, it had no appeal in Europe, where women culturally spent less time styling their hair at home.

Meanwhile, the high cost of manufacturing meant the rollers came with a price tag that American women, who loved the concept, weren't willing to pay. In the end, Clairol had a fantastic product that couldn't gain traction in either market.

This issue highlighted a much bigger problem: Clairol's product development maze. Riddled with obstacles—from cultural mismatches to a rigid structure forcing unsuitable products into every market, the system didn't just hinder progress, it eroded morale. Employees grew frustrated as they watched resources poured into products destined to fail. It was a recipe for stagnation and stifled innovation.

The first step in fixing this maze was clear: address the disconnect between the teams. Over time, barriers had developed that were as personal as they were procedural. European managers had grown accustomed to viewing their American counterparts as overly US focused, prioritizing domestic sales—which accounted for 75 percent of the appliance division—at the expense of understanding international markets.

Meanwhile, the Americans often dismissed the Europeans as overly critical. Without bridging this divide, meaningful progress would remain out of reach.

To break the impasse, I brought everyone face-to-face, for the first time. The goal was simple: help people see each other as individuals, not stereotypes of their homelands. Around the same time, teleconferencing technology was becoming a game-changer, and we embraced it fully. It bridged physical distances, enabled real-time collaboration, and helped break down cultural barriers.

Discovering great talent within an organization during a turn-around is incredibly rewarding. As I assembled teams and met with people across our European branches, I encountered several exceptional individuals who truly stood out.

One person who really stood out was Fiona Harrison, our head of marketing. Fiona was outstanding at her job. She had the knack of understanding the market and connecting with consumers. I could see her potential right away, but wanted to watch her closely because I had a hunch she could do even more.

In 1985, when I was given responsibility for Clairol Appliances Worldwide, we immediately promoted Fiona to run the European side of the business. She was the obvious choice. She had the skills, the instincts, and the understanding of the market we needed.

Promoting her was one of the best decisions I made. Fiona was superb in the role, and her leadership helped take our European business to the next level.

The next step was centralizing new product development under my leadership. Previously, it had been fragmented across international divisions, which only added confusion and inefficiency. By bringing it all together, we sent a clear message: innovation was our top priority.

To support this shift, I formed a new products committee with twenty members representing regions and markets worldwide. This committee became the heartbeat of our innovation efforts, meeting monthly to resolve conflicts and clear roadblocks quickly, no more drawn-out delays.

One breakthrough was giving international market managers the power to reject products that didn't fit their business needs or cultural context. For the first time, they had a real voice in the process. It was a huge step toward building trust and collaboration.

We also shifted to a more flexible approach to product design. Instead of forcing the same products into every market, we started with core ideas and adapted them to meet European regional preferences.

Take hairdryers, for example. Internally, they all used the same reliable engine, but the exteriors were customized for different markets. European consumers wanted sleek, stylish designs, while American buyers valued functionality and durability. By tailoring the aesthetics without reinventing the product, we efficiently met the needs of both markets.

These changes transformed the way we operated. We became a collaborative organization where international teams worked together, while local managers retained the freedom to refine their product lines. The structure encouraged risk-taking with new ideas—some succeeded brilliantly, while others flopped. But with our newfound agility, we could quickly pivot: advance the winners and scrap the rest.

It wasn't perfect, and we learned plenty along the way. But this new structure let us innovate faster and with greater confidence. What had once been a disjointed maze transformed into an organization capable of decisive action and adapting to diverse markets worldwide.

As a turnaround CEO, fixing the maze, the decision-making structure, is always a top priority. In a struggling business, slow decisions can be fatal. You need to act fast, which often means tearing down the old maze and rebuilding it from the ground up.

The new maze has to strike a balance: structured enough to keep everyone informed, but flexible enough to enable swift action and collaboration. Bottlenecks, redundancies, and outdated processes have to go, replaced with a system that works for the business, not against it.

Ultimately, the goal is to empower the team to move decisively, react in real-time, and stay aligned with the company's direction. When you get this right, the organization becomes nimble, responsive, and ready to move forward.

TECHNOLOGY CAN'T DOMINATE COMMUNICATIONS: FACE TO FACE IS BEST

Communication has always been convenient for the X-Men superhero team. Their leader, Professor Xavier, could use telepathy to contact each member even if they don't have cell service. Likewise, technology has become essential for business communication, offering efficiency and instant connectivity although we haven't figured out the telepathy part (yet!).

However, in my opinion, nothing can truly replace face-to-face interaction, which remains unmatched in building relationships and fostering effective communication.

Since the early 1990s, email has been the backbone of business correspondence, providing a reliable way to exchange information, though it can be misinterpreted due to the absence of vocal tone and physical gestures.

Instant messaging platforms like Slack and Teams enable real-time collaboration and integrate seamlessly with productivity tools, but they can also lead to information overload and disrupt focus.

Video conferencing tools such as Zoom and Google Meet restore the visual element, fostering personal connections—especially vital after the COVID-19 pandemic's shift to remote work. However, while video calls help bridge communication gaps, they often feel less engaging due to connection issues, delays, or the awkwardness of speaking to a screen. There's also always the temptation to be distracted by things off-screen.

Ultimately, no digital tool can replicate the depth of connection achieved through in-person interactions. The nuances of body language, the energy of a shared space, and the informal conversations that naturally happen during in-person meetings all play a crucial role in building trust and strengthening individual and professional relationships.

Recent studies suggest that reducing face-to-face interactions in business can negatively impact creativity and productivity. Research highlighted by the MIT Sloan School of Management underscores the critical role of face-to-face communication in driving innovation. In their study, *The Returns to Face-to-Face Interactions: Knowledge Spillovers in Silicon Valley*, economists David Atkin (MIT), M. Keith Chen, and Anton Popov analyzed smartphone geolocation data alongside patent citations to quantify the impact of in-person interactions. They found that even modest reductions in face-to-face contact can significantly hamper innovation. For example, a 25 percent drop in direct meetings could lead to an 8 percent decline in patent citations, a key indicator of innovative output. The findings offer compelling evidence that proximity and real-time collaboration are not just beneficial, but essential, for fostering breakthrough ideas (MIT Sloan, 2023). Insights from Stanford GSB echo the MIT findings: in-person teams outperform virtual ones in creative collaboration. In *Thinking Inside the Box: Why Virtual Meetings Generate Fewer Ideas*, researchers Jonathan Levav (Stanford) and Melanie Brucks (Columbia) found that pairs working face-to-face generated 15–20 percent more ideas than those collaborating over Zoom.

They discovered that virtual communication restricts eye-gaze and cognitive breadth, essential components of spontaneous, associative thinking, and often imposes structured turn-taking that stifles dynamic back-and-forth exchange.

Together, these studies from Stanford GSB provide clear evidence that in-person teams benefit from immediate, unstructured idea flow, allowing team members to build on each other's thoughts in ways that virtual environments typically inhibit.

Virtual communication, while essential for maintaining connections over long distances, often lacks the emotional depth and satisfaction of in-person interactions. Without physical presence, subtle but crucial nonverbal cues—like body language and tone—can be missed, making relationship-building more challenging.

Perhaps this is why business travel has largely rebounded, at this point in time, to pre-pandemic levels. According to a February 11, 2025, *Investopedia* article, Marriott International reported that global occupancy rates have surpassed 2019 levels, though travel from Monday through Wednesday remains lower, likely due to flexible work policies. Even as digital tools improve, professionals still recognize the irreplaceable value of face-to-face interaction in fostering stronger connections.

As we navigate the complexities of global business communication, balancing digital efficiency with personal engagement is key. Scheduling regular in-person meetings, organizing company retreats, or even opting for a phone call instead of an email can add clarity, strengthen relationships, and enhance mutual understanding—ensuring that technology remains a tool for connection rather than a barrier.

Reflecting on my experiences, especially in international contexts, I've seen how reliance on technology can sometimes widen the chasm of miscommunication. For instance, American colloquialisms in emails and texts can easily confuse an overseas factory owner. Yet in person, even without words, body language conveys meaning, and over the phone, nuances in tone and demeanor help bridge gaps—elements missing in typed messages.

I experienced this firsthand during a trip to China, where tensions had been created due to miscommunications in emails. Prioritizing efficiency over clarity, our brief messages failed to fully express our intentions and respect for our partners. It wasn't until we met in person—sharing tea and conversation—that I could properly convey our stance and apologies. The shift was immediate; understanding replaced frustration, and the partnership was strengthened.

That experience reinforced my belief that while technology is invaluable, it must be balanced with human interaction. When possible, nothing compares to the clarity and connection achieved through direct meetings.

As leaders, our goal should be to use technology as a tool to enhance—not replace—genuine communication. By doing so, we not only avoid miscommunications but also foster stronger, more respectful international relationships.

Choosing the optimal method for communication in any setting, whether personal or professional, is crucial for effective interaction. Here are three steps I use to help determine if I've selected the best method for my communication needs:

1. **Does it fit the goal?** Think about what you need to accomplish. For example, if the goal is to make a quick decision, a phone call might be more effective than an email. If the purpose is to brainstorm ideas, an in-person meeting or video conference might be better to facilitate dynamic interaction and collaboration. The right communication method should directly support what you aim to achieve.

2. **Feedback and Engagement Levels:** I like to watch how people react and what kind of feedback you get. The best communication methods really draw everyone in, letting them actively participate and share their thoughts. For example, if a video call sparks lively discussions and team problem-solving, it's probably doing a better job than

emails that get ignored or just lead to more questions. This way, you can see which methods truly engage your team and keep things moving smoothly.

3. **Efficiency and Clarity:** Given the importance of communications, always evaluate the efficiency and clarity of the interaction. The optimal method should convey messages clearly and without unnecessary complexity or delay. It should reduce the risk of misunderstandings and ensure that information is received and understood by all parties as intended. If you find that messages are often misinterpreted or require frequent follow-ups for clarification, it may be time to reconsider if the communication method is the best choice.

By keeping these checkpoints in mind, you can make sure your communication hits the mark every time, keeping things smooth and straightforward.

Again, I'm reminded of Iron Man, aka Tony Stark—a genius inventor who relies on high-tech armor and gadgets to operate globally. Yet, despite his dependence on technology, many of the most pivotal moments in the Marvel Universe happen face-to-face.

In both comics and films, key Avengers meetings and strategy sessions take place in person, not over screens. Even Stark, for all his technological prowess, recognizes the importance of gathering the team physically. These direct interactions foster better teamwork, clearer communication, and stronger trust among the Avengers.

This mirrors the real-world value of face-to-face communication in business and leadership. While digital tools are invaluable for staying connected, they can't fully replicate the depth and nuance of personal interactions.

Just as the Avengers thrive through in-person collaboration, real-world meetings cultivate engagement and stronger working relationships, proving that even in a digital age, nothing replaces human connection.

BE A CHEERLEADER: ALLOW OTHERS TO DREAM

Captain America is one of Marvel's most famous superheroes, but he's known for far more than just his fighting prowess and indestructible shield. In fact, Cap is Marvel's ultimate leader. Throughout comics and movies, he uplifts and inspires his team, no matter what dangers the Avengers are facing. He also serves as a mentor for characters like Spider-Man and Bucky. As leaders, we all need to be like Captain America.

Throughout my career, I've learned that successful leadership hinges not just on strategic adjustments or financial restructuring, but overwhelmingly on nurturing an environment where innovation thrives. Leadership is less about issuing commands and more about being a cheerleader; it's about encouraging and inspiring everyone to dream and innovate.

My approach has always involved painting a vivid picture of the future, not with vague promises but with detailed, strategic plans. For example, discussing a blueprint to expand into new markets with my teams—not just as possibilities but as actionable items with identified targets.

This vision wasn't just about growth for the sake of expansion but about strategically leveraging our strengths in new and impactful ways. We'd identify specific regions where our products could succeed, setting concrete goals without getting lost in the minutiae of exact figures.

Creating such an environment was crucial. It went beyond keeping the team content—it was about making them feel secure in the current plan and excited about the future. This culture of empowerment and trust allowed us to innovate continuously, critical in sectors like consumer products where success often hinges on the next big idea.

For instance, leading teams at Black and Decker, I emphasized an open environment where everyone could pitch ideas, no matter how unconventional. At Remington, a suggestion to explore rotary shavers—a departure from our traditional foil shavers—initially seemed impractical but eventually marked a significant breakthrough, showcasing the power of encouraging and embracing unexpected ideas. The business leaped forward, and it wouldn't have been possible without the supportive leadership environment.

As a CEO, I found that real change was achieved not through formal announcements or written memos but through the consistent, visible behaviors that encouraged an open, collaborative, and innovative workspace. It meant stepping back and allowing others to take the lead, trusting in their capabilities and being there to support rather than to direct every move.

Leaders must articulate a clear and compelling vision, not through commands but through conversations that engage and inspire their teams. This involves transparent communication about the company's goals, strengths, and areas for improvement, making every team member feel they are part of a shared journey.

I've learned that fostering a culture of risk-taking is essential, yet it must be balanced with accountability. This isn't about recklessness; it's about cultivating an environment where daring to innovate is encouraged and failures are seen as part of the learning process.

Reflecting on this, there were times when a well-thought-out risk didn't pan out. As a leader, it's crucial to accept that not every risk will lead to success. I believe that if you're taking ten risks, succeeding in seven or eight is a triumph. It's about understanding that the failures are just as valuable as the victories. They provide critical lessons that refine our strategies and strengthen our resolve.

Handling failures involves being upfront about the realities of risk. For instance, in the consumer products sector, the dynamics of risk are considerably different than in the creative industries like motion pictures. In both arenas, however, the principle remains the same: embrace risk judiciously, support it with solid research and preparation, and fuel it with breakthrough ideas.

Take Marvel, for example, when we decided to start our own movie studio—a decision that was initially met with skepticism both inside and outside the company. This wasn't a wild gamble but a calculated strategy to enhance our control over our characters and their stories.

We didn't come to that decision lightly. We'd spent years apprenticing with the big studios—Sony, Fox, Universal—learning the business of blockbuster filmmaking while producing Marvel's early hits. Sony had Spider-Man, Fox had X-Men, and Universal had the Hulk. Each character landed where they did, not by strategy, but because not every studio truly *understood* every character. And that mattered to us. These weren't just assets—they were personalities with decades of legacy. No matter how sweet the deal, we always chose the studio that "got it."

We often initiated the talks, but once we sat down, they had to show us they understood the character's soul. No one was going to make a great film about a hero they didn't fundamentally understand.

Eventually, we looked around and said, "We've learned all we can. Let's do it ourselves."

That shift wasn't about ego; it was about experience. We had been hands-on with production, script approval, casting. And we saw the inefficiencies up close. The big studios had massive backlots, lavish offices, and layers of overhead. Marvel Studios? Just thirty people in Beverly Hills.

We didn't need soundstages; we could rent them anywhere. We didn't need luxury; we needed efficiency. The old system was bloated. Ours would be lean, focused, and disciplined.

David Maisel, an industry veteran with a sharp eye for opportunity, was the one who'd led the initiative. "We've learned enough. We can do it better. We can do it cheaper." And he was right. At its core, a film is just a team of skilled professionals brought together to execute a vision. That's how the studios did it. And it's exactly what we planned to do.

Our first big swing was *X-Men 1*. Wolverine, the franchise's breakout character, was the focus, and the studio system wanted a star. I remember agents pushing for Tom Cruise, costing millions up front, plus back end.

But we had a different philosophy: the *character* is the star, not the actor. We didn't need box office draw, we needed authenticity. So, we cast a relatively unknown Australian song-and-dance man named Hugh Jackman. More economical. And he *was* Wolverine.

That was the start of Marvel Studios. Not born in a boardroom, but forged in decision after decision where we bet on story, character, and conviction over convention.

We weren't just making movies anymore. We were rewriting the playbook.

Similarly, the idea of revisiting and retelling origin stories for iconic characters like Spider-Man and the Hulk was initially controversial. But after careful analysis and a clear understanding of the market, the strategy proved to be a resounding success—drawing in a whole new generation of fans. In my role, whether it was advocating for innovative ideas at Marvel or emphasizing product development at Black and Decker, I strived to ensure that creativity was never stifled by fear of failure. It was about making clear that our future depended not just on the safe bets but also on our willingness to venture into uncharted territories.

Moreover, a leader must ensure the organization hires individuals not only for their skills but for their potential to embrace and enhance this culture of empowerment. It's about forming teams that are diverse in thought and united in purpose, capable of moving the company forward in innovative ways.

I've always leaned into my nature as a risk-taker. It's fundamental to who I am—an optimist at heart, always ready to take on challenges that many wouldn't dare to consider. I call it my "adventurer gene." This trait has defined my approach to leadership and has been crucial in navigating the often-tumultuous waters of reviving companies.

For instance, my decision to apply to Harvard Business School was driven more by a challenge than a genuine expectation of getting in. Despite encouragement from my ship's captain and some very senior navy officers, I remember thinking it was a long shot—maybe even a waste of time. But I went ahead anyway. It wasn't the risk of failure that held me back; I didn't even see it as a real risk because my expectations were so low. The real challenge was getting past the mental barrier—the belief that it was out of reach. In a way, that mirrors how I've approached turning companies around ever since.

In leadership, you often find yourself in scenarios where the conventional path won't cut it. You need to be bold, but more importantly, you need to instill confidence and a sense of security in your team. It's about showing them that it's okay to think outside the box, to bring seemingly wild ideas to the table because those are the ideas that can change the game.

One moment that tested that approach came during our early push into what we then called video games, I was especially eager to move quickly—capitalize on the Marvel brand's momentum and stake our claim in an expanding market. But I held back. Instead of dictating direction, I chose to let the team find the best path forward. I gave them room to evaluate opportunities and make the key calls. That autonomy didn't just build their confidence—it deepened their ownership of the project. And when it succeeded, it validated something I've always believed: capable people thrive when you trust them to lead.

Philosophically, that's how I approach leadership. I like to push decision-making down into the organization—and I expect the people who report to me to do the same with their teams. That cascading confidence creates a more agile and accountable culture. Most of the time, I'm happy for those teams to handle the day-to-day decisions without coming to me for approval. But there are a few types of decisions where I stay involved.

First, I need to be at the table for what I call policy decisions—anything that changes the rules of the game. If a call is going to shift the way we operate or set a precedent across the organization, I want a say in that. Second, I stay close to decisions that affect multiple functions. For instance, if finance is making a move that impacts marketing or operations, I expect them to loop everyone in—and I'll usually weigh in myself. It's not about control; it's about cross-functional awareness. You can't have one department making waves that ripple through the rest of the company without coordination.

Finally, there's the money. I set a dollar threshold—above which I want to be informed. That amount varies depending on the size and maturity of the organization. In some companies, it might be $1 million for any single purchase, whether it's inventory or equipment. In larger organizations, that number might be much higher. And when I'm new to a company, I purposely set that threshold low. It gives me insight into the flow of decisions and helps me get my arms around the business. Over time, as trust builds, I raise it—and that in itself becomes a powerful gesture. It shows people, in a tangible way, that I believe in their judgment.

That's how you build leadership throughout an organization. Not by controlling every move, but by setting the parameters, staying engaged in the big things, and letting talented people run.

And when things didn't go as planned, I didn't pass the buck. Acknowledging my role in these setbacks was crucial—it's what a leader does. I've always believed that if a project fails, the blame should not fall on the team alone. As the leader, I had endorsed their plan, so the failure was as much mine as theirs.

This perspective extends to successes as well. When we achieve success, whether it's launching a new product or improving our financial standings, I make sure the credit is distributed fairly. More often than not, these successes are the result of collaborative efforts, involving contributions from various departments and team members. Acknowledging this collective effort is essential. In public settings, particularly when discussing the achievements of a public company, I've always emphasized that every employee plays a part in our successes.

Reflecting on leadership, I've realized a critical truth: success might have many parents, but failure is indeed an orphan. This axiom echoes through every decision I make, highlighting the responsibility I carry as a leader to both inspire and protect my team.

During my career, I've always emphasized that as the leader, I bear the ultimate responsibility for failures. This approach not only reduces the fear of failure among my team members but also fosters an environment where they feel safe to take risks. For instance, if a project doesn't pan out as expected, I wouldn't single out individuals but would take on the mantle of failure myself. This gives my team the freedom to innovate without the paralyzing fear of repercussions for honest mistakes.

Such a stance is crucial when it comes to balancing guidance with autonomy. Initially, in any new role, I find myself offering more direction while I learn who on the team can handle more responsibility.

Over time, as trust builds, I gradually begin to delegate significant decisions. For example, in meetings, I might publicly back a decision by a team leader, effectively signaling to the entire organization that I trust their judgment. This not only empowers them but also boosts their credibility within the team.

This empowerment can lead to remarkable transformations. Nothing gives me quite the sense of satisfaction as when I see a team thrive after being given the autonomy to solve problems. It's like watching a well-coordinated orchestra perform flawlessly without needing to intervene—it's exhilarating and affirming. This dynamic has repeatedly confirmed my belief that the right mix of trust and autonomy can turn potential failures into great successes. It's these moments that fuel my passion for leadership and make all the challenges worthwhile.

This approach to leadership—focusing on being supportive rather than solely directive—has not only enabled the companies I've led to navigate through turbulent times but has also prepared them for future challenges long after my departure. This legacy of empowerment is what truly defines successful leadership—it's not just about the battles fought but also about the groundwork laid for enduring success.

ESSENTIAL #14

CELEBRATE SUCCESS PUBLICLY

At the conclusion of the blockbuster Marvel film *Guardians of the Galaxy*, Star Lord leads his team in a celebratory dance as they soar off into space, having once again saved the universe. Even those who once dismissed his dancing skills join in the public celebration. Star Lord demonstrates a key understanding: a collective celebration with his entire team holds far more significance than personal recognition.

In my own experience as a CEO, I learned that recognizing people's efforts—whether with praise or tangible rewards—can significantly boost a company's culture, especially in an environment that values innovation and risk-taking.

I remember a tough turnaround phase at one company, where money was tight, but I still wanted to make a difference. So, I called an all-hands meeting and publicly handed out checks to one team who contributed to a particularly successful project. The checks were small, but honestly, that simple gesture meant a lot. It showed everyone in the room that their hard work, no matter how small it seemed, really mattered.

I've always looked for excuses to celebrate success, no matter how small. Take throwing a Christmas party and inviting spouses for the first time, or celebrating a major milestone with beers in the warehouse. I remember one quarter when we shipped more product than ever before, and we gathered everyone together for a casual toast right there on the floor. Those moments weren't extravagant, but they mattered. They showed people that their hard work was seen, appreciated, and worth pausing to celebrate.

That same mindset applies to innovation, too. Failure is part of the process. Take, for example, someone who might have launched several unsuccessful new products but still managed to deliver more hits. It's those successes that should be recognized, not the number of failures. In my view, a truly innovative environment thrives on a steady stream of ideas, with a solid business structure in place to quickly evaluate whether those ideas have potential, financially and otherwise.

But here's the thing: it's important to focus on the positives and not get bogged down by the negatives. Failures should be analyzed for lessons, then left behind so the team can stay motivated and keep morale high. That said, if someone is failing consistently, it usually points to a lack of competence, and they need to be let go. The danger is sending the message that failure is acceptable, which can drag the whole organization down.

Celebrating successes publicly in the workplace offers numerous benefits, as supported by various studies and articles. A Gallup study, highlighted in the article "The Importance of Employee Recognition: Low Cost, High Impact," found that employees who do not feel adequately recognized are twice as likely to say they'll quit in the next year, compared to their recognized peers. *Better Humans*, a self-improvement publication, echoed this in a post discussing the finding, emphasizing how public celebrations not only boost motivation but also strengthen team cohesion and foster a positive workplace culture. Additionally, such celebrations are not only about acknowledging individual achievements but also about strengthening bonds among team members, reinforcing a sense of communal success. This can increase employee retention and satisfaction by making team members feel valued and appreciated.

Recognizing achievements can help align the entire organization toward common goals, nurturing a supportive and vibrant work culture that attracts both current employees and potential new hires. It also offers a moment to reflect on what has worked, turning those successes into learning opportunities for future projects.

However, embedding this dynamic attitude into corporate culture doesn't happen through words alone—it requires consistent, action-oriented leadership. For example, regular bonuses for innovative efforts can be a great incentive, but it's essential to avoid fostering a cutthroat environment where individual achievements are overly emphasized. Instead, a collaborative atmosphere where consensus is valued leads to more sustainable innovation and helps prevent the pitfalls of haphazard, individualistic endeavors.

Several major companies, such as McDonald's, Bank of America, Google, and Walmart, have built strong cultures around recognizing success and celebrating employee contributions. These organizations have developed robust internal programs that not only honor individual achievements but also reinforce their commitment to recognition and reward across the company.

For example, McDonald's honors exceptional performance with the Ray Kroc Award, given to the top 1 percent of managers. This prestigious award includes a cash prize, a trophy, and a trip to the awards gala, showcasing their dedication to excellence and leadership in the service sector.

Bank of America fosters a culture of recognition and inclusivity through various employee networks. These networks offer leadership development opportunities and engage employees in community service, aligning celebrations with both business strategy and community involvement. The company also recognizes employees through formal awards, such as the Global Volunteer Awards and the President's Volunteer Service Award, which acknowledge significant volunteer efforts, emphasizing the importance of contributions both inside and outside the workplace.

Google has a comprehensive recognition system, including the "gThanks" program, where employees send "thank you" notes to their peers. This program is woven into their performance feedback and career development processes, cultivating a culture of appreciation. Additionally, peer-nominated awards offer monetary rewards and stock options, significantly boosting employee motivation and productivity.

Walmart's approach to recognition is deeply integrated into its corporate operations, with public acknowledgments and awards at key company events. Their "Live Better U" program offers employees opportunities for professional advancement without the burden of debt, encouraging personal and career growth. Walmart also emphasizes promoting from within and features employees in national advertising campaigns, further demonstrating its commitment to employee development.

When it comes to celebrating success, there are several effective strategies to consider:

1. Promote Inclusivity: Acknowledge everyone involved in the success, including members from different departments if the achievement spans multiple areas.
2. Diversify Celebration Methods: Not every success needs a grand celebration. Sometimes, a personal thank-you note, highlighting someone's efforts in a team meeting, or a small team gathering can be just as meaningful.
3. Nurture Peer-to-Peer Recognition: Encourage employees to celebrate each other's accomplishments. This strengthens team spirit and helps break down traditional hierarchical barriers.
4. Connect Celebrations with Company Culture: Ensure that recognition aligns with your core values. This reinforces the company's mission and highlights the significance of each achievement.

Regularly celebrating achievements can significantly boost morale and align team efforts toward shared goals. These celebrations are vital for nurturing a strong organizational culture, filling the workplace with resilience and vibrancy.

Balancing encouragement with accountability, as well as individual recognition with team collaboration, has not only helped guide companies through challenging times but has also set them up for sustainable success well beyond my tenure.

As the saying goes, *it's just as important to enjoy the journey as it is to reach the destination,* and every achievement along the way deserves recognition. This approach to leadership focuses on laying the foundation for a culture that doesn't just survive but thrives through collective effort and shared victories.

TRY TO SELL YOUR IDEAS TO SUBORDINATES. DON'T RAM THEM THROUGH

Let me paint a typical picture for you.

As I walk into the conference room for my first meeting with the senior team at a struggling company, I am acutely aware of the tension that awaits me. The company has been losing ground to competitors, and morale is understandably low. This isn't just another day at the office; it's the start of a critical turn-around effort.

The air is usually thick with anxiety. Glances are exchanged—some wary, others outright nervous. These executives are grappling with uncertainty, fearing job losses, drastic changes, or both. Despite this palpable concern, my purpose here isn't just to shake things up; it's to steady the ship at the same time. These are opposing challenges.

I'm not overly concerned with reading body language or analyzing every crossed arm or raised eyebrow. Sure, I notice the room's energy, but my main focus is gathering information. People are often stiff at first, sitting there with their arms crossed, waiting to see what I'm all about. That's normal. It's not every day someone new walks in to assess the lay of the land. But that tension eases over time.

"Selling your ideas to a team during a crisis is as much about tone as it is about content," I often remind myself. Rather than bulldozing through the meeting with a list of immediate upheavals, I aim to instill a sense of calm amidst the storm.

We all know exactly what's at stake and where the hard conversations will probably lead, but I don't want to show any hint of panic or extreme emotion. My goal is to set a clear, steady tone. I start by openly acknowledging the challenges, not to alarm anyone further, but to pave the way for honest and open dialogue. We discuss past shortcomings and, more importantly, focus on potential strategies and innovative solutions that could drive recovery.

Once the word gets out that our meetings aren't confrontational or tense, people start to relax. I don't come in swinging or targeting individuals—it's just not my approach. Those first few days might not be the most productive because everyone's still figuring the new guy out, but as we meet with groups multiple times, sometimes four or five times in that first month—the conversations become more open. People start to share more honestly, and I can ask better, more informed questions. It's a process, and that's okay.

By fostering a dialogue rooted in transparency and collaboration, I am trying to transform initial fears into a unified commitment to turn the company around. It's about demonstrating that, while the path ahead will be tough, it is navigable with the right approach and team effort. This is how you begin to change the dance of a company's culture, from a disjointed sequence of panic moves to a strategic, synchronized ballet that revives and sustains.

I'm candid about the obstacles we face, while also emphasizing that I'm not tackling them alone. Their help is needed, and we're in this together. The first meeting isn't about me dictating solutions; it's about establishing trust, engaging their perspectives, and showing, through both words and demeanor, that we'll tackle the challenges as a team.

After the first month of deep listening, something always shifts. By then, we've sat through countless meetings, asked what feels like a million questions, and I have absorbed as much as one possibly can. It's during this phase that the big picture starts to come into focus. I start to see the bottlenecks, the inefficiencies, and the opportunities for change become obvious to all. That's when I start transitioning from listening mode to action mode.

One of my priorities at this stage is to act decisively, but never recklessly. For example, I've often found that marketing and advertising are areas where a lot of improvement can be made quickly. If an agency isn't delivering quality content, I don't hesitate to make a change.

It's not a hasty decision; it's based on observed outcomes. When I've replaced advertising agencies, I've consistently seen not only immediate improvements but also more impactful campaigns. These new ads are memorable and more effectively prompt consumers to purchase, often at a lower cost.

The common mistake in advertising is equating memorability with effectiveness. Just because an ad is the talk of the Super Bowl doesn't mean it will boost sales. Effective advertising should do more than catch the eye; it must compel the consumer to act.

That's why, in my turnarounds, I prioritize consumer testing for advertisements. Running focus groups isn't just cost-effective; it's a direct way to gauge if an ad can sell the product, not just make it memorable. My approach is straightforward: produce advertisements that don't just stick in the memory but drive consumers purchase. Wins like that not only build momentum but also show the team that we're serious about raising the quality of our reputation with customers.

Beyond marketing, I dive into the product pipeline. I want to know what's in development, why the team believes it will resonate with customers, and whether it's aligned with the market's needs. If something feels off, I push the team to rethink it. My approach isn't to critique for the sake of critiquing but to encourage sharper thinking and better alignment with business goals.

Manufacturing is another key focus. I often ask questions like, "Why are we still assembling this in-house? Could we streamline costs by outsourcing?" or "What are our competitors doing, and how do their strategies compare to ours?" These aren't throwaway questions. They're designed to spark strategic thinking. Sometimes the answers confirm we're on the right track. Other times, they reveal opportunities we've overlooked.

Now, here's the thing about asking these kinds of questions: they inevitably signal change. People start to realize I'm probing for a reason, and that can create some unease. That's where my leadership style becomes critical. I've always believed in the power of quiet confidence.

When I address the team—whether it's a department or the entire company—I stay calm and steady. My tone is measured, my body language relaxed. I want them to feel that, yes, we have challenges, but they're solvable. It's not about panic; it's about urgency with clarity and purpose.

Building trust is the cornerstone of this process. By the time I start making significant changes, people have seen me in action. They've watched me sit through hours of meetings, genuinely listening to their concerns and ideas. I don't just tell them I care—I show it through my actions, my questions, and my willingness to engage. That trust makes all the difference. It's what allows people to embrace change rather than resist it.

This approach has been consistent across every turnaround I've led. It's not about being flashy or dramatic. It's about being deliberate, thoughtful, and clear-eyed, even when the stakes are high. Change, especially in a crisis, is never easy. But when it's rooted in trust and delivered with quiet confidence, it becomes not just manageable—but transformative.

Of course, resistance is always a factor in a turnaround. You expect it. But I've found it doesn't usually show up in dramatic ways. No one's standing up in a meeting and yelling, "That's never going to work!" or questioning why I'm there. Resistance is subtler—it's

in what people don't say or in a certain hesitation during a conversation. Early on, I'm not looking to call it out. I'm focused on
setting the tone and establishing trust, not starting battles.

One of the ways I work to build that trust is through communication, overcommunication, to be precise. I know some leaders
prefer a *need-to-know* approach, keeping information tightly con-
trolled. It's efficient, but I've never found it to be the best way to
engage people. I believe that when people feel connected to the
broader organization, they perform better. They don't need to be
involved in every detail, but they should feel included in the bigger picture.

For instance, if I'm leading a marketing meeting, I'll often
include salespeople, even if sales isn't the focus. Marketing decisions, like advertising campaigns, directly impact their work, and
they usually have great insights. A salesperson might mention that a
customer loved a recent campaign for a product, or they might flag
something that didn't resonate. That kind of feedback is invaluable,
and it shows the team that their input matters.

This approach is about more than just gathering ideas—it's
about culture. By opening up these conversations to people from
different parts of the organization, we're building a sense of ownership. When people see their insights influencing decisions, they
feel valued. And when they feel valued, resistance starts to give way
to collaboration. That's how you begin to shift the culture from the
inside out, and it starts with listening, overcommunicating, and fostering an environment where everyone feels like they have a stake
in the outcome.

If I'm in a quality control meeting, I want people from manufacturing there, maybe even someone from sales and marketing.
Why? Because quality isn't just about the product, it's about how
customers perceive it, and that's a conversation worth having across
functions. Sometimes, the quality is fine. But in many cases, it's
not, and the problem often stems from the fact that these teams
aren't talking to each other. It's shocking how often I've seen

this—functions working in isolation, issues never surfacing, and no one connecting the dots.

Dysfunction often stems from poor leadership—leaders failing to foster collaboration or encourage communication between teams. That's why I bring people into meetings who might not typically be involved. For instance, the guy running product quality doesn't need a vote on advertising agencies, but being part of the discussion broadens his perspective and breaks down silos. Silos thrive under exclusivity, but I've always believed in overcommunication. Including more voices creates engagement and alignment, far outweighing the efficiency of keeping meetings small.

I've seen the power of inclusion firsthand. At one company, the culture was so fractured that employees who'd worked just fifty feet apart for years didn't even know each other. Hosting informal pizza lunches helped change that. Simple introductions and the sharing of war stories built strong connections, and those connections transformed how people worked together. When teams know each other, they collaborate better—it's that simple.

Sometimes, team members would thank me for including them in a meeting, even if their presence wasn't essential. It showed them they were valued, reinforcing why overcommunicating isn't just a strategy—it's the right thing to do. Inclusion fosters purpose, and that drives real change. The more people feel involved, the more invested they become. And that's the foundation of any successful turnaround: making people feel like their voice matters.

In many real-world leadership situations, decisions have to be made without all the information you'd ideally want. Whether you're launching a new initiative, navigating shifting market conditions, managing a team, or simply moving fast in a dynamic environment, uncertainty is part of the job. That's why I'm upfront early on and say, "We'll be making decisions with incomplete data. Mistakes will happen—I'll make mistakes—but I'll own them, and we'll fix them together." I also make it clear: "If you want to get in trouble with me, don't bring me problems, or let me keep heading down the wrong path without speaking up."

Of course, trust isn't built with words alone; it's built with actions. Over time, people see how a leader operates. When I misstep, I own it. I don't dodge responsibility; I'll say, "All right, I blew it. Let's figure out how to fix it." That vulnerability helps build trust because it invites partnership, not just obedience.

Building trust takes time, especially when it comes to team members feeling comfortable pointing out a leader's mistakes. Sometimes it's weeks or months before someone feels safe enough to say, "Peter, I think you got this one wrong." When that happens, I see it as a win—it means trust is taking root, and that's the real cultural turning point in any organization.

Occasionally, someone will challenge decisions I've made, especially in speeches or communications. They might say, "I think you misjudged so-and-so's role," or, "You shouldn't have taken that advice." When people feel comfortable enough to raise those concerns, I take them seriously. I don't dismiss their input, even if I don't always agree.

Most major decisions in turnarounds are joint efforts, but there are times when I've had to push something through, even if it wasn't popular. I hate the idea of "ramming something down people's throats," but sometimes urgency demands it. The key is transparency—explaining why it's necessary. Even if people disagree, they'll respect you if you're clear and respectful.

Speed and decisiveness are critical in turnarounds, but you have to pair them with humility. Admitting and swiftly correcting mistakes isn't a weakness, it's a strength. When you involve your team in fixing errors, you don't lose trust; you earn it.

At the same time, urgency often dictates action. We don't always have the luxury of endless debate—we sometimes must quickly reach a decision and move forward. I remember when I was in the appliance business, where timing around gift-giving seasons like

Christmas and Mother's Day was everything. Products had to be on retailers' shelves, backed by promotions, on a tight schedule.

For instance, we once had a new hairdryer that needed to hit stores by September. The team was stuck debating something as basic as the color. White, beige, black? Time was running out, and we couldn't wait any longer.

So, I made the call. I picked a color, and off we went. The sales force pitched it, but the feedback came back: customers didn't like it. Valid reasons poured in, it didn't pop on shelves, showed dirt easily, or just looked wrong in the packaging. Back then, even black wasn't a good option; it simply didn't sell.

The moment the issue arose, we jumped on the phone with the manufacturing team in Hong Kong. "We need to change the color to beige," we told them, basing the decision on customer feedback. We tackled the problem immediately, and the team saw that I wasn't afraid to admit the mistake and fix it to meet deadlines. These kinds of decisions weren't uncommon—in seven turnarounds, we probably handled a hundred potential disasters like this.

The bigger decisions, though, were different. Take moving manufacturing to Asia. I've made that call five or six times, and it's never easy. Asking a team to find overseas vendors means they know US factories and long-standing vendor relationships are on the line. Sometimes, these vendors were friends, relationships built over years. Now, I was asking my team to tell them, "We're moving this business overseas." It wasn't easy for anyone.

In those moments, I always acknowledged how tough it was. "This isn't personal," I'd tell them. "It's about survival. If we don't make this move, we can't compete." I couldn't handle the legwork myself, but I made sure they understood the necessity. Over time, they saw the results—cost savings, better margins, and the ability to reinvest in the business.

Decisions that disrupt lives and relationships are never easy, but in a turnaround, they're part of the job. The key is to face them head-on, with transparency and urgency, while staying human in your approach.

Empowering people has always been a priority for me. It's about involving them in decisions that make their voices feel heard, even when the choices are tough. For instance, picking partners—whether it's an advertising agency, a supplier, or a distributor overseas—requires inclusivity.

In smaller European countries like Portugal or Denmark, you need local partners because the market isn't big enough to justify your own presence. Sometimes, long-term partners no longer fit, and changing those relationships is hard, especially for employees with strong ties to them.

I always made it clear to the team that I understood the difficulty of breaking those relationships. There's an emotional toll, but I ensured they felt part of the process, not just dragged along. That involvement helped them feel ownership over shaping the future.

Inclusion also meant involving people from different divisions in meetings—marketing, sales, quality control, or warehouse operations. Breaking silos fosters collaboration and creates a culture where people feel invested.

Morale plays a huge role in a company's success. While you can occasionally use surveys to gauge sentiment, they're not always reliable, and anonymity and honesty can be tricky. For me, the real indicators were in the numbers: if the company was performing well, it meant people were motivated. Beyond that, I leaned on simple, human gestures to boost morale, things that didn't cost much but made a big difference.

But keeping morale high isn't just about celebrations, it's also about clearing the roadblocks to action. The issue is rarely a lack of understanding; it's a lack of follow-through. Maybe people have been ignored, or they're afraid to speak up. Even in good companies, people avoid controversy. That's where leadership steps in: creating an environment where action feels safe and supported.

When it comes to making decisions, especially in high-pressure situations, I've relied on a mix of instinct and data. Data is critical, but in turnarounds, you don't always have the luxury of extensive research—you've got to trust your intuition. That said, I've never made a major move completely against the board, investors, or the broader leadership team. If I ever found myself that isolated, it was a sign I needed to reassess. But I've absolutely made tough calls when key functions or departments disagreed.

Take sales and marketing. Sales might insist an account will carry more product if pushed, while marketing argues the advertising won't drive demand. Or there's a debate over pricing: should we focus on quality or volume? These disagreements are normal, but someone has to make the call—and that's where a leader steps in. My team knows I value their input, but I'm also mindful of time. We can't debate forever. If I'm wrong, we'll fix it. Most disagreements aren't catastrophic—they're just part of the process.

Leadership isn't about forcing change or throwing your weight around; it's about earning trust, bringing people together, and getting everyone invested in the process. From the first meeting to the final decision, success depends on listening, overcommunicating, and creating an environment where people feel valued, heard, and empowered to contribute. Whether it's tweaking a plan based on feedback, breaking down barriers between teams, or making tough calls with transparency and respect, the key is leading with calm confidence. Real change doesn't happen when ideas are forced, it happens when people believe in them. That's what great leadership is all about.

EMBRACE TRUE EMOTIONAL MATURITY

There's a long list of superpowers enjoyed by Marvel superheroes. Here's one you won't find—"super maturity." In fact, the super-heroes journey of achieving emotional maturity is central to the plotline of many popular Marvel movies and comics.

The best example is again, Tony Stark, aka Iron Man. Stark begins his career as a superhero with the same immaturity he displayed as a business tycoon. Vain, self-centered, arrogant, and willing to use his billions to paper over his transgressions.

But throughout the *Avengers* movies he gains emotional maturity and evolves into a leader. His superpower isn't the nuclear reactor implanted in his body or his Iron Man suit, it is his selfless devotion to his team. It turns out we can all learn a lot from Iron Man!

Usually, by the time I arrive at a company in need of a turn-around, the leadership team is long gone. But there was one time when the CEO was still there when I walked through the door. He'd been at the company for thirty years, with half of that time spent as the company's leader.

I remember the moment clearly—he was waiting for me in his office, and I could tell he was ready to pass the torch. What struck me most was his honesty. He wasn't defensive or trying to save face. Instead, he said, "Peter, I'm glad you're here."

At first, I didn't believe him. His words felt like a polite gesture, but I knew what it meant. My arrival was a clear sign that his time was up. Yet, he continued, "You will do the things I couldn't. I couldn't fire my friends."

That moment stuck with me because it encapsulated the harsh reality of leadership in challenging times. In smaller or older companies, especially those with a familial culture, it can be incredibly difficult to make tough decisions, particularly when those decisions involve people you've known for years. The kind of leadership needed in those situations often requires a level of detachment—something that can feel like a betrayal to the personal connections built over decades.

This is where true emotional maturity comes into play. Leadership isn't just about making the right decisions for the company; it's about understanding that those decisions can hurt others. It's about accepting that personal connections won't always be enough to keep the company afloat. Sometimes, you must prioritize the health of the organization over personal loyalty. This takes emotional strength because it means making the difficult choice to let go—not only of familiar faces but of the emotions tied to those relationships.

Remember, we're not talking about the normal ups and downs of business here. Turnaround situations are existential crises—and failing to let go of people who feel like friends or family can sink the entire ship.

In those moments, a company needs a steady, dispassionate hand—someone willing to make the hard calls required to save it. That often means layoffs, salary cuts, slashing benefits, even moving from high-end offices to more modest spaces. And the truth is, some people who were at those companies when I made those decisions still aren't fans of Peter Cuneo to this day.

I've had to make those calls in every one of the seven turnarounds I've led. Each time, the pressure comes from all directions.

Employees, suppliers, banks, customers—they all have their own expectations, and they're waiting for you to act. Suppliers want payments, banks are holding loans that have been neglected too long, and customers are fed up with poor-quality products or services. As a turnaround leader, you're not just cleaning up internal messes—you're also answering to external forces that won't wait.

It's a delicate balance, and the pressure can feel overwhelming. But one thing I've learned is that you need to be prepared for this pressure before you take on a turnaround role. It's not for the faint of heart. Every decision you make will be scrutinized, and there will always be those who disagree. At least you know going in that you're jumping from the frying pan into the fire, which is much better than finding out on your first day.

Outstanding leaders are often remembered for making decisions that weren't popular at the time. History is full of leaders who were initially criticized for their choices but ended up reshaping their companies, their countries, or even the course of history. They could see the bigger picture, understanding that the short-term consequences might be tough, but that the long-term impact would prove them right.

Take Abraham Lincoln, for example. When he became president, the country was on the verge of civil war, and his opposition to slavery made him deeply unpopular in many parts of the nation. The decision to fight the war and preserve the Union wasn't easy, and it came with a huge cost. He faced intense criticism, but he held firm in his belief that the nation could not survive half slave and half free. His choices, including the Emancipation Proclamation, were divisive and controversial, but they ultimately preserved the United States and changed the course of history. Today, we look back and see that his leadership, though unpopular with some at the time, was nothing short of transformative.

The same principle applies in business. Leading a company through a turnaround often means making bold moves that others won't immediately understand. One great example is Steve Jobs when he returned to Apple in 1997. At the time, Apple was on the brink of collapse, weighed down by a bloated and confusing product lineup. Jobs made the bold and widely unpopular decision to slash 70 percent of Apple's products, narrowing the focus to just four: a consumer desktop (iMac), a consumer laptop (iBook), a professional desktop (Power Mac), and a professional laptop (PowerBook). The move caused panic—employees feared layoffs, and investors worried Apple was shrinking into irrelevance. But that streamlined focus improved product quality, clarified Apple's vision, and ultimately set the stage for its legendary resurgence with the iPod, iPhone, and beyond.

Just as Lincoln's leadership preserved the Union through painful but necessary choices, Jobs's unpopular decisions laid the foundation for Apple's comeback. In both cases, doing what's right for the long term mattered more than doing what was easy—or popular—in the moment.

Leadership is about maturity. It's understanding that no matter what, you can't make everyone happy. Sometimes, your personal popularity must take a back seat to the bigger goal. If you're serious about leading, that means making tough decisions, even if they don't win you any favors.

Now, let me be clear: I'm not talking about being a jerk just for the sake of it. Some leaders take pride in their abrasiveness, almost as if being labeled a "bastard" is a badge of honor. That's not the kind of leadership I mean. A strong leader doesn't intentionally upset people for power's sake.

Instead, a strong leader is aware of the emotional landscape of the team, sensitive to their needs, and communicates consistently to reduce uncertainty. People need to feel informed, even when the news isn't good. Keeping communication open, especially when things are tough, is crucial.

But here's the key: while it's important to be attuned to your team's emotions, a strong leader will never let emotions dictate their decisions. You're there to do a job. The decisions you make may not be popular in the moment, but they need to be right for the company's long-term health. You're not there to win a popularity contest; you're there to save the company.

If you're stepping into turnaround leadership, you have to come to terms with this reality: you will make lifelong enemies. There are people I've had to let go or whose visions didn't align with the direction the company needed to go, and they've been talking about what a terrible person I am ever since. Ten years later, I still hear it. They've kept my name alive in their stories of how I ruined their careers or made their lives miserable. Frankly, I really don't care.

But once you've made the decision to step into a turnaround role and accepted that you can handle the heat of tough decisions and widespread resistance, there's another, equally important reality you need to face: the impact it will have on your personal life.

Turnaround work isn't just difficult in the office—it spills over into every aspect of your life, especially your family and friends. You may think you're prepared for the long hours and relentless pressure, but the reality is, you won't fully understand how much it will affect those closest to you until you're in the thick of it.

A turnaround is inherently a crisis, and crises demand all of your focus and energy. When you're in it, your work becomes an obsession. It will demand every ounce of your attention, and at times, it will consume you in ways you never imagined. Long hours are just the beginning. Even when you're physically at home, your mind is still at the office. You may try to switch off, but the truth is, it's impossible. Your mind will constantly race through strategies, problems, and decisions.

The work is all-consuming. And here's the tricky part: when you're home, you're often not totally *there*. You might be sitting on the couch, pretending to watch TV, but in reality, you're replaying scenarios or solving problems that are waiting for you at the office the next day.

I faced this challenge even at a time where it was much easier to unplug. As a turnaround executive in the current day, you'll be facing unending pings on Teams or Slack, constant Facetime or Zoom video calls, and perhaps even desperate stakeholders tracking your location via your smartphone!

I'll never forget how frustrating that was for my wife. For years, she would talk to me, and she could tell I wasn't always listening. She'd say something, and I'd nod along, but my mind wasn't engaged. It must've felt like I was ignoring her—or worse, pretending to pay attention.

But the truth was, I wasn't even paying attention to the TV. I wasn't present at all. I was mentally working through the crisis I was managing, and that frustration—her frustration—was something I could never truly make up for.

I'd go to bed feeling like I'd let her down. Still, there was always a voice in my head telling me I could find a way to balance my personal and professional lives. But the truth is, that balance was rarely there.

Then, there was the constant upheaval of moving. My career in turnarounds meant relocating my family several times, often in quick succession. We lived in New Jersey, Canada, California, and Connecticut. Each move meant new schools for our boys, new neighborhoods, and my wife had to rebuild her social circle. Every time, it felt like starting over. It was tough on everyone, especially my wife, who shouldered much of the emotional burden while I focused on the company and the crisis at hand.

Looking back, I realize I wasn't always the husband or father I wanted to be. I couldn't give my family the attention they deserved because the work often came first. The pressure to succeed was so intense that most everything else became secondary. I believed I was doing what was best for my career—and ultimately, for my family—but it was hard to ignore the toll it was taking on my relationships.

What I've learned from those years is that no matter how noble you believe your cause to be, you can't ignore the people who matter most. They bear the brunt of your decisions and distractions.

And when it comes to family, the sacrifices for work often don't show rewards right away. It takes time for them to understand, and sometimes they never fully will. But if you're going to do this kind of work, you have to accept the balancing act—tough decisions and sacrifices. The real challenge is finding a way to lead in the office without losing yourself or your family.

One of the most valuable courses I ever took at Harvard Business School was called The Executive Family, taught by the school psychiatrist. It was one I took with my wife. The course was designed to help executives like me navigate the delicate balance between personal and professional life.

It was an eye-opening experience. My wife and I were forced to sit down and really think through the difficult questions—questions that, at the time, felt like distant possibilities but that would soon become our everyday reality. When would we have children? How much time would I be away from home? How often would I be traveling?

These weren't just hypothetical scenarios. These were the very issues we'd have to confront once I finished school and stepped into my career. The course helped us lay out a roadmap for how we would navigate those decisions together—encouraging us to be proactive rather than reactive when the inevitable conflicts between personal and professional goals arose. The course was incredibly valuable—but I didn't fully take its lessons to heart when it mattered most.

And those conflicts *did* come up—again and again. There were days when I was incredibly unpopular at home. My focus on work, the long hours, constant travel, and the pressure of managing business crises all took a toll on my family.

But through it all, I was lucky. I had a wife who, despite the difficulties, always rallied around me. She never once hesitated to stand by my side. I know that sounds simple, but when you're in the midst of a turnaround and you're giving so much of yourself to a business, it's easy to take your loved ones for granted. But I couldn't have done any of it without her.

When the chips were down, and everything seemed to be falling apart, I could always count on her to carry me through. She understood the bigger picture. She understood that these sacrifices, while painful in the moment, were necessary for the long-term stability of our family and for my career.

But not everyone is so fortunate. When you choose a high-intensity career path, you need to ask yourself an important question: Do you have a support network that can withstand your absence, or even better, stand behind you despite it? The reality is, in demanding roles, your personal life will sometimes take a back seat. There may be times when your family feels like an afterthought. You'll miss school plays, family dinners, weekend trips. And it's during those moments that your support network will either hold you up, or struggle under the weight of your absence. As I look back on my journey, I can't help but be thankful for the lessons I learned—both from my career and from the people who stood by me. The road to success in any demanding role is tough. It's filled with sacrifices and compromises, but also meaningful rewards. And none of those rewards would have been possible without the unwavering support of my family.

So, if you're considering a high-pressure role or an intense career path, take a moment to reflect on what it might mean for your personal life. Ask yourself if you have a network of people who will be there for you when the going gets tough, and whether you're willing to make the sacrifices necessary to keep that support strong. Because no matter how successful you become in your career, it's the people who stand by you through it all that will make the journey worthwhile.

In the end, emotional maturity isn't just a leadership trait, it's a life skill. And the deeper your well of maturity, the steadier your hand will be when the storms inevitably come. But its value goes far beyond managing conflict or handling strain at home.

Emotional maturity helps you make clear decisions under pressure, separate ego from judgment, and respond, not react, when things go off course. It allows you to listen openly, communicate with empathy, and adjust when feedback challenges your assumptions. It's what keeps a leader calm in crisis, grounded in uncertainty, and resilient through change. And it shows up in the small moments, pausing before speaking, owning your mistakes, giving credit freely, and remembering that leadership isn't about being right, but about getting it right.

ESSENTIAL #17

ELIMINATE LAYERS OF MANAGEMENT THAT EXIST ONLY TO PASS DATA FROM ONE LEVEL TO ANOTHER

One of the most important questions in any organization is deceptively simple: Do we really need to fill that position at all?

Early on, I made the same mistake many leaders make. When key people left, say, a VP of marketing and a VP of sales, the instinct was to replace them both. It feels responsible, even urgent. But I learned that's not leadership. That's maintenance.

In many cases, the smarter move is to pause and ask: Can one exceptional person do both jobs? I've done this more than once. We'd hire someone with range, someone truly capable, and pay them maybe 75 percent of the combined salaries. Not only did we reduce cost, but we also eliminated a layer of potential miscommunication. The result? A leaner team, faster decisions, and better outcomes.

What I didn't fully grasp early in my career is just how much unnecessary weight organizations carry. So many roles exist purely to push data from one level to the next, without ever making real decisions.

In one company, we had eight vice presidents doing work that, realistically, required four. We made the change, and the four who left were forgotten within a month. That was my wake-up call: headcount isn't impact.

And here's another counterintuitive truth: the best people for a turnaround often aren't the ones with the shiniest résumés.

Conventional hiring logic says you want polished professionals, the sales superstar, the marketing guru, the spreadsheet-slick product manager. But those people often struggle in chaotic, fast-moving environments. They've been conditioned to operate within structure. In a turnaround, that structure is usually broken, or nonexistent.

The people who thrive in those moments are rarely "perfect" on paper. I once hired a product development lead who missed internal check-ins, couldn't keep up with documentation, and made traditional managers nervous.

But he could build. He could see around corners, invent what customers didn't yet know they needed, and move the company forward. In a conventional setting, he would've been managed out. In a turnaround, he was a game-changer.

You need people who don't just work the system, they challenge it. Who see bureaucracy for what it is: a tax on momentum. People who care more about progress than optics. People who redesign the rules while others are busy following them.

If you try to hire in the image of a large, established organization, you'll miss the mark. You're not a Fortune 500 company, you're building something lean, focused, and adaptive. Hire accordingly. Look for builders, not maintainers. Problem-solvers, not process-fillers.

And while you're streamlining your team, take a hard look at how information flows too. Many organizations are buried in reports, data, memos, updates, dashboards, created to meet needs that may no longer exist. At Marvel, my partner, Ike Perlmutter, had a brilliantly simple way to test their value: just stop sending them. No warning, no explanation. If no one noticed, it wasn't useful. If someone asked about it, you'd found the few who actually relied on it. Those people went on a short list. Everyone else? Cut the clutter.

It's a simple principle: hire with intention, communicate with purpose, and constantly question what adds real value.

Much like in the movie *Wall Street*, when Gordon Gekko questions what half the vice presidents at Teldar Paper actually do besides send out useless reports, I've often found the same, layers of people who exist to transmit information that has no impact.

Whether it's people or paperwork, anything that exists solely to move data from one desk to another without adding insight or action is a drag on performance, and it has to go.

Cutting that noise has a measurable effect, not just on efficiency, but on morale. People appreciate clarity. When you strip away the unnecessary, everyone can focus on what truly matters.

Because in the end, paper doesn't fix companies. People do.

MAKE SERIOUS CHANGES ALL AT ONCE—IF POSSIBLE

Remember that moment in the first *Iron Man* when Tony Stark, fresh out of captivity, holds a press conference and stuns everyone by announcing Stark Industries is out of the weapons business?

The room goes still. Eyes widen. His CFO nearly chokes. No one saw it coming.

That's what bold change looks like. It hits hard. It rewrites expectations. But if you do not back it up with clarity and trust, it backfires fast.

Because real transformation is not just about making noise; it is about showing people what comes next.

When I walk into a company that is struggling, whether it is Marvel or any other brand I've worked with, the clock starts ticking the moment I step in the door. There's no easing into it.

You aim to stabilize, build trust, and start turning the ship. Fast. In that order, if you can.

People are looking at me like, *Okay, what's he going to do?* And that is fair. Their livelihoods are on the line. The organization's future is on the line. The tension is real. So, the very first thing I try to do is give them a sense of the road ahead.

I want people to feel like we're going to work intensely over the next three months to figure out what changes need to be made. And I'm intentional about the way I say it: "about three months." Not four weeks. Not six months. About three months.

That phrasing matters. People are scared. And I've learned that uncertainty is toxic. If you do not give people a framework for how change is going to happen, it starts to feel like Chinese water torture—just this endless drip of anxiety. So, I try to frame it in a way that feels manageable. Something they can get through. Something they can believe in.

Now, do I always wait the full ninety days to start making changes? No, I do not. In fact, in most cases, I start making changes sooner. But giving people that ninety-day window creates some breathing room. It gives me time to assess the situation clearly, and it gives them time to mentally prepare.

What people often do not realize is this: making all the big, serious changes at once is really difficult. It sounds great, clean, surgical, like ripping off a Band-Aid. But in real life? It's rarely that simple. Not because I do not know what to do. Not because I'm hesitant. It's just the logistics. The day-to-day realities of how businesses actually operate. That's where the real complexity lies.

Let me give you an example. Changing your advertising agency is one kind of decision. Moving your manufacturing overseas? That's a completely different kind of move. They operate on totally different timelines. The processes involved, the dependencies, the contracts, it is like comparing apples and jet engines.

That said, if the conditions are right, *really* right, there's power in making bold moves all at once. It creates clarity. It sends a signal: we're serious, we're moving forward, and this is not business as usual. It rallies the organization and resets the energy.

But let's be honest, that kind of alignment is rare. The timing has to be right. The resources in place. The organization ready. And above all, the communication airtight.

So while the textbook version of change might look like one clean sweep, most of the time it's a balancing act. You move fast where you can. You sequence what needs space. And you keep your people in the loop, because no matter how strong your plan is, it's your people who bring it to life. Or not.

It's very difficult, almost impossible, to implement sweeping changes all at once. Each function, each department, has to be evaluated individually. You can't just walk in and say, "Let's cut 15 percent across the board," and call it a day. That's not leadership. That's laziness wrapped in a spreadsheet.

You have to understand how each department actually works. Where there's flexibility. What can truly be cut, and what can't. What looks easy on paper is often far more complex in practice. That's why I never treat departments as interchangeable boxes on an org chart. I treat them like ecosystems. And ecosystems need different things to stay healthy, especially under pressure.

In turnaround work, this is common. I'll have departments where there are no cuts at all, zero. And right down the hall, another one with major cuts. That's just the nature of the beast.

You go one by one. You take the time to understand what's really happening, what makes sense, where there's room to move, and where there isn't. It's not a blanket process. It's tailored. It's detailed. And it takes time.

Which is why this idea, that you can do everything at once, is more of a goal than a guarantee.

Early in my career, I did treat it as a goal. I didn't want to say outright, "Hey, this is impossible," because the moment you do that, people stop taking it seriously. They let themselves off the hook. But over time, you see the pattern.

And that is where structure comes in. Because when you are in a situation where multiple things need to happen and resources are limited, you need a method. You need a way to prioritize. A system to sequence your moves. Otherwise, you are just making noise.

That's where the discipline becomes really important. It's not just about evaluating departments in isolation; it is about looking at the business holistically. Understanding which changes are going to be complex and require time, and which ones can be done fast. Some changes seem like they should be quick, but they're not. They're loaded with complexity—contractual, cultural, technical. You cannot just make an announcement and expect it to materialize in five minutes.

And then on the other end of the spectrum, there are things that really can happen in five minutes. You pull a lever, make a call, change a pricing model, reassign a team. Boom. Done.

That's part of the art of this work, knowing which is which. Reading the play. And acting accordingly.

And through it all, communication is everything. Everything. You have to communicate properly, clearly, consistently. You have to be honest. You have to show up in front of the organization and speak like a human being, not a press release.

You never make a promise you cannot keep. If you do not know the answer to something, say exactly that: "I don't know." And say it straight. People respect that more than any polished, scripted non-answer. Because in moments of uncertainty, honesty becomes a stabilizer.

You can't lie—not even to make people feel better in the moment. The minute you start lying—or even sugarcoating—it backfires. You may be well meaning. You might want to give employees a sense of relief by saying, "We'll have all the changes done by X date."

But if you miss that date? You break that trust. And now the employees are saying, "Well, this guy's full of it." They were counting on that date, holding on to it like a lifeline. And when it passes without answers, they lose trust. They stop believing you know what you are doing. And that is a killer in a turnaround.

I've seen this play out firsthand.

That kind of trust, or lack of it, was something I walked right into at Marvel. I didn't know comics. I didn't know movies. And in that world, especially the movie world, perception matters, a lot. People weren't shy about questioning my credibility. Not as much in comics; that crew was more grounded. But in film? Power dynamics and image ruled the day.

And that shaped how I communicated. I had to be clear. Direct. Unflinching, but calm. Because in high-stakes environments, people are constantly reading between the lines. They're looking for signs of strength, of control, of vision. When you are leading through change, how you show up matters as much as what you say.

Which brings me back to this whole idea of making rapid changes, ripping the Band-Aid off. People ask me all the time, "Was there ever a moment where you made a big decision and saw results right away?"

Honestly? No. Not really.

Nothing important happens instantly. Everything meaningful takes time to see. You lay people off to cut costs? Okay. But those same people are getting severance. Sometimes for three months. Sometimes for six. If they are senior, maybe nine. You do not actually feel that cost reduction right away—it could be half a year before it hits the bottom line.

So no, there's no next-day payoff. Not in the kind of work I do. And that is something leaders need to internalize. If you're doing this work because you're chasing a quick result, you're in the wrong line of business. Real transformation is measured in months, sometimes years, not minutes.

And once those hard changes are made, once the layoffs are done, the org chart redrawn, the vendors shifted, the real leadership work starts. People are bruised. They're uncertain. They're wondering if they are next.

That's when I double down on communication. Because it does not stop once the hard conversation is over. In fact, in many ways, it becomes even more important.

When someone asks me if more changes are coming, I do not make false promises. I say what I know. "I'm not aware of any." That's not a dodge; that is me being truthful. Because even when the big waves are over, the ripples remain. People need reassurance. They need time. They need consistency.

So, keep talking. Keep showing up. Celebrate minor wins. Call out positive momentum, even if it is small. Because all of that helps reinforce a new culture.

That's what you are doing at that stage. You're not just fixing a business. You're reshaping how it thinks. How it behaves. How it believes in itself. Every message, every meeting, every decision, it's all reinforcing the culture you're trying to build. And you build it not in big speeches, but in small, steady acts of leadership, repeated every day.

There's no shortcut for that part. No announcement that can substitute for it. Culture doesn't come from the top down; it comes from the inside out. And people don't just listen to what you say; they watch what you do. They watch how you show up when things are hard. They watch how consistent you are, and whether your words match your actions.

And over time, if you're clear, if you're consistent, if you keep showing up and telling the truth—momentum builds. Doubt fades. Hope sneaks back in. You start to hear laughter in the halls again. People start suggesting ideas, not just executing orders. They stop asking, "Are we going to be okay?" and start asking, "What's next?"

That's when you know it's working.

Because the real win isn't just saving the company, it's building something better than what was there before. Something stronger. More resilient. More alive.

And while you'll want that shift to happen fast, it never does. The early days are everything. Your people need decisive leadership from day one. They need to see movement. Direction. Stability.

That's the work. And it's not for the faint of heart. But if you get it right, you don't just turn the ship, you set a whole new course.

ESSENTIAL #19

BE RUTHLESS WHEN CALLED FOR

The Avengers are locked in a life-or-death battle with forces bent on destroying the Earth when Loki, the villain who thinks he's the smartest being in the universe, comes face-to-face with the Incredible Hulk. Sneering, Loki tries to talk his way out of trouble: "I am a god, you dull creature!" But the Hulk has other ideas.

Without a word, the giant green hero grabs Loki by the heels and smashes him into the ground, over and over. The villain is left wheezing, stunned, and humiliated, while audiences of all ages erupt in laughter.

It's one of my favorite scenes in *The Avengers*, not just because of the reaction, but because there's a leadership lesson buried in it: when arrogance meets real power, talk doesn't cut it. In high-stakes situations, decisive action matters.

Unfortunately, when an organization starts to drift, ethics often erode alongside performance. It's usually a sign that leadership has lost its focus, its integrity or both.

I compare it to an abandoned building that's burned to the ground. The fire may be dramatic, but it's the rot underneath that fed it. Once the structure's gone, rebuilding becomes nearly impossible; you're left with a shell and no support. That's why, when you step into a broken organization as its new CEO, you don't start with hope or team-building exercises. You start with a knife. You cut out the rot, and then see what's still strong enough to build on.

Make no mistake: change isn't gentle. It demands clarity, urgency, and when it's called for, ruthlessness. You may have to take a page out of the Incredible Hulk's book.

By the time you arrive, many of the high-quality people are already gone. What's left is a group of checked-out employees who look around and think, "This place is going nowhere but down. Doesn't matter what I do, no one cares anyway." Even senior staff can lose their edge. They get comfortable, self-interested, numb to the decay.

Your job is to snap them out of it. To make it clear: that ends today. You care. You're in charge. And you're willing to make hard, uncomfortable moves to prove it.

Marvel made superhero movies, not westerns, but I liken this to the moment in a classic western when the hero walks into town and says, "There's a new sheriff in town." That line isn't about ego, it's about accountability. It signals that someone is finally watching.

And if you really want to send that message, you need to know where to look first. It took me a while to learn this, but in a turnaround, there are a few places you always check right away. Purchasing is one of them.

Over the years, I've seen incompetence, carelessness, and sometimes, something worse. I don't make accusations lightly, but when someone refuses to share basic purchasing data, it raises red flags. Why hide what should be routine?

The truth is, purchasing is one of the easiest areas to exploit if no one's watching. It's simple to set up a shell company, issue invoices just under approval thresholds, and quietly siphon money. The amounts are small, the pattern looks normal, and auditors rarely catch it.

That's the danger. It's not the big scandals that sink companies, it's the constant drip-drip of smaller problems. I've seen it happen more than once. And the people behind it? They always justify it. "It's harmless." "No one will notice." And for a while, they're right.

That's why, in a turnaround, I look at purchasing first. Not because I expect bad actors, but because it's the easiest place for them to hide. And when trust is fragile and every dollar counts, you can't afford rot at the center.

If you're leading through crisis, don't start with the org chart. Start with the money. Follow it closely. The culture you build begins with what you're willing to question.

Sometimes, though, culture doesn't shift with a memo; it shifts with a sweeping, public display of resolve that makes everyone sit up and take notice.

I once had problems in a warehouse, too. A few employees were stealing inventory, but everyone else working there knew and looked the other way. Fear and indifference kept them silent. We inserted a detective posing as a new employee. Within a week, I had a full list of names.

Now, I could've fired them quietly. But that wouldn't have shifted the culture. So, I brought in the local police to arrest them on the spot, right in front of everyone. Then I addressed the team: "I know you knew. You're all responsible. If anything else goes missing, none of you will have jobs."

Guess what? Theft stopped immediately.

You could see it in their faces, the guilt. They couldn't even make eye contact. And honestly, they were probably decent people who'd just gone numb in a toxic environment.

That's why I preach zero tolerance for ethical lapses. Not just because it's right, but because it works. Everyone working under me needs to know: I live by that code.

Of course, when you start making real changes, you'll face resistance, especially from those who thrived under the old, broken system. These are the ones who put self-interest first. Whether they're

stealing from your warehouse or cashing checks while playing soli-
taire, they'll drain your momentum. And you don't have time for that.

Find them. Let them go. Fast. You won't need to clean house
twice.

As I noted in essential #3, another zero-tolerance issue for me is
sexual harassment. It's disgusting. It's unacceptable. And yet, it's still
far too common.

A few weeks into a new job, two female executives came to my
office to complain about their boss. He'd been harassing them for a
while. They'd stayed quiet until I simply asked, "What's going on?"
Just giving them space to speak brought the truth out.

I confronted him. He admitted it, laughing. He confessed grab-
bing women's legs under the conference table. Thought it was
funny. I fired him on the spot. Everyone knew exactly why.

Actions taken outside the US sometimes draw comments. "Our
culture is different. We're more relaxed about this than Americans." I
said, "Bullshit." You don't get to hide behind culture when it comes
to basic human decency. Sexual harassment is wrong. Everywhere.
Period.

That's what it means to be ruthless when it's called for. When
someone crosses a moral or ethical line that clearly, there's no room
for ambiguity. Whether or not you have final authority, you can still
take decisive action, flag the issue, escalate it, or hold firm to the
standard in your sphere of influence.

In some cases, it may involve partnering with HR or senior
leadership to make the consequences clear. The key is that people
see the line, and understand what happens when it's crossed. That
clarity is essential to a healthy culture. And it can be the difference
between lasting progress and quiet erosion. Of course, not every
situation is so clear-cut. Cultural differences can create gray areas.
I had one of those moments back in the 1980s, during a visit to a
vendor in Hong Kong. After dinner, we did some window shopping on the way back to my hotel. I casually mentioned a watch I
liked, but said it was too expensive.

The next day, I returned to my room, and there it was, gift-wrapped. That same watch, along with a note wishing me luck and expressing hope for our future business.

In many Asian cultures, a gesture like that is standard and seen as a positive expression of goodwill. But in my world? It walks a fine line; it can easily be perceived as a bribe.

I didn't want to offend them, but I couldn't keep it either. So, I accepted the gift, but made it clear it belonged to the company, not me. Later, we gave it away in an office-wide drawing.

Different situation. Same principle. When the ethical lines blur, you still act decisively, and in a way that sends a message. People are always watching. Make sure what they see reflects the standard you expect. People take their cues from what the organization tolerates, and what it won't.

I've told that story many times. Some people say I should've sold it and donated the money. Maybe. There's more than one right answer. But I'll always choose the one that clearly demonstrates, publicly, that I take ethics seriously.

From the dock loaders to the boardroom, every single person under you needs to see that you are a person of integrity, and that you expect the same of them.

Now, ruthlessness? It's necessary. But use it sparingly. Too often, and you'll breed fear, not excellence.

Some infractions aren't as obvious but are just as corrosive, like laziness.

At one company, we formed a new strategy committee with people from every division to brainstorm fast-track, revenue-generating ideas. We needed momentum. But one individual kept stalling. He was responsible for bringing essential reports to each meeting, and every time, he showed up empty-handed, offering flimsy excuses. My displeasure was obvious to everyone in the room.

He finally got the message. The next day, he quit. It was for the best; he was blocking progress. I didn't revel in it. I never do. These moments are uncomfortable, but they matter. You can't be afraid to call someone out when their behavior undermines the mission. Sometimes, the way you handle one person sets the tone for everyone else.

That said, your actions should always be proportional to the breach. Leadership isn't about throwing your weight around, it's about protecting the culture and, in some cases, the survival of the organization. Not everyone around you will play fair. Some might come after you if it helps them climb the ladder. So stay alert. Keep your guard up.

I once started in a new senior job in a division of a large company. My boss and secretary seemed above board. My wife and I attended a company gathering. She came away convinced they were having an affair. I laughed. No way. A month later, I got a 3 a.m. phone call from my boss's wife, in a panic. She couldn't find him. Okay, maybe my wife was right.

A week later, my boss walked into my office and told me to promote my secretary to an open position. Now, this woman was nice enough, but she was a high school grad. The job required an MBA. It was absurd. I refused to do it. I realized then that he wasn't just unprofessional, he was unethical. From that moment, we were on the opposite side of the table.

Soon after, I moved to corporate HQ. And what do I hear? He's trashing my performance. Trying to kill my career.

I went to top management and laid it all out. They were shocked, and they backed me. His reputation tanked. He traded everything for her, but it didn't last. Surprising no one but him.

But I took two lessons from that:

First, don't ignore pessimists. I tend to see the good in people. But optimism without realism is dangerous. My wife saw what I didn't.

Second, when someone's coming for you, act fast. If they don't share your values, or the company's mission, they're a threat. Cut them loose.

That's what leadership demands. Ethics. Clarity. And, when the moment calls for it, ruthlessness. You step into the wreckage, make the hard calls, and protect the people who are still committed.

In that sense, I've always felt a little like Nick Fury, the eye-patched strategist who built the Avengers. Not the guy with powers, but the one who assembles the team, clears out the corruption, and sets the mission. He doesn't care if you like him. He cares if you're ready to fight for something better. So do I.

90 PERCENT OF BUSINESS PROBLEMS ARE BASED ON POOR LEADERSHIP

I've always believed that 90 percent of problems, whether in business, nonprofits, or other fields, are rooted in poor leadership, particularly in confusing *management* with true leadership. It's easy to think that every challenge can be solved by textbook business strategies, but reality often tells a different story.

In my experience with turnarounds, what really made a difference wasn't just what looked good on paper. It was about rallying the team and leading them out of tough times into brighter days. That's the real key to ensuring a turnaround sticks and leads to lasting success.

Ironically, it was most often a shortfall in past leadership that had led the company into those dark times to begin with. Anyone can seem like a leader when the going is easy and everyone's happy. The true test of leadership comes during the tough times; that's when you really see if someone has the emotional stamina to steer the ship.

Being a leader isn't just about making the popular choices; it's about having the guts to make tough calls that might not win you any popularity contests. It means putting your words into action, being a consistent presence, and standing strong even when others falter around you.

A lot of failures boil down to confusing *management* with *leadership*. To me, management is what you do with *things*, like a warehouse, equipment, bank accounts, or a spreadsheet. These things won't question your decisions. But *leadership*? That's about inspiring people, guiding them to achieve great goals. People will question what you tell them. When you're just starting out, managing might dominate your role. But by the time you're a CEO, leadership needs to be 95 percent of your job.

As chief executive, it's crucial not to get bogged down in every little data point. Leave that to your team. Your primary role is to shape the company culture, refine the structure, and ensure that the right people are in the right positions to drive the vision and address organizational strengths and weaknesses.

Many executives, however, fall into the trap of failing to adjust the balance between managing and leading as they ascend the corporate ladder, often resorting to micromanaging and losing sight of the broader vision. Successfully shifting from managing to leading, which involves blending intuition with knowledge and adapting your approach to fit the situation, is challenging but critical, it's what distinguishes truly great leaders.

Let's look deeper into how leadership dynamics can play out, using the hedge fund boom as an example. Back then, executives who were great at crunching numbers and making analytical decisions suddenly found themselves leading teams of eager, ambitious young professionals.

These teams weren't just looking to advance the fund; they were also keen on moving their own careers forward. But here's the problem that many of these executives struggled with and that was the transition from individual contributors to leaders. As these firms grew at breakneck speeds, those who climbed the corporate ladder quickly found themselves unable to adapt.

Instead of empowering their teams by delegating analytical tasks, they got insecure doing the math themselves. This not only left their young teams directionless, slowing down decision-making and leading to misguided investments, but they also failed to demonstrate the essential leadership quality of trust in their team's capabilities. This oversight can erode respect, which is crucial for effective leadership. A financial firm with directionless analysts is in trouble as bad as a comic book company short on artists, and I've seen both firsthand!

Effective leadership is about more than just making decisions; it involves connecting with your team on a personal level, showing them that they matter and understanding their perspectives. This is how leaders earn respect, not merely through holding a C-suite title but by proving their worth and reliability to their teams. This approach not only enhances decision-making but also builds a robust, supportive work environment.

This principle of leadership was vividly brought home to me during my time in the Vietnam War, serving as one of the air intercept controllers aboard the USS *Strauss*. In this role, I was responsible for monitoring aircraft from nearby carriers, providing pilots with critical location information once they were beyond their home carriers' radar range.

My call sign, Fleet Fox, comes from Admiral Joseph Strauss, the pioneer of mine warfare in the US Navy. Besides leading the Asiatic Fleet between the World Wars, Strauss worked in the Bureau of Ordnance within the navy, where he developed several significant naval weapons, including the superimposed system of mounting guns, the first spring recoil gun mount, and the first disappearing mount for submarine deck guns. His focus on clear, direct communication and mutual respect influenced my own leadership style, especially in high-stakes conditions.

During this time, I'd travel by helicopter from our guided missile destroyer to an aircraft carrier to discuss tactics and threats with the pilots. On one such occasion, the pilots suggested I experience the back seat of a navy Phantom (F4-E) jet during maneuvers. This wasn't just a joyride; it was a chance to truly understand the demands I was placing on these pilots when I directed high-G turns and supersonic speeds.

Little did I know, this experience would also test my own resilience in a way I hadn't anticipated. The pilots had planned a bit of a prank to see if I could handle the pressure, or more accurately, the nausea. They figured if I managed the ride without losing my lunch, I'd prove I had "the right stuff." There was no way I could decline without losing face.

Officially, having a non-trained person like me on such a flight was a big no-no, but we were a hundred miles from enemy territory, just circling around the carrier. We catapulted off the deck, hitting 150 mph in about four seconds, then shot vertically into the sky in afterburner mode. It still amazes me today how these pilots can handle being launched at breakneck speeds, manage their tasks, and then land on what's essentially a floating strip of metal.

The Phantom aircraft, a dual-engine beast capable of exceeding Mach 2 (twice the speed of sound), dipped just below flight deck level before picking up speed over the ocean. It's an incredibly powerful yet agile machine, one of the best ever built. The Phantom was versatile, serving both as a dogfighter and a light bomber.

We shot up about ten thousand feet and then plunged into a nosedive, followed by a series of high-speed turns and maneuvers. Despite wearing a G-suit to alleviate the stress, I had no training on how to properly use it. For most of the flight, my eyes were shut tight; I clung on for dear life. I swear I thought my head would burst as I battled fiercely against the overwhelming urge to throw up.

We weren't far from the *Strauss*, maybe fifty miles out, when the pilot asked if I wanted a quick aerial view of my ship. I said yes without thinking. We skimmed several hundred feet above the water, approaching the *Strauss* "on the deck." Over the radio, the pilot cheekily announced, "Fleet Fox, this is Tip Top 44 coming for a visit with your boy."

We buzzed the bridge at just under Mach 1, an act as against navy regulations as anything I could even imagine. Later, folks on the bridge told me the roar was so loud and unexpected, it left them dazed with their ears ringing for a good while after. Later in life, a scene in *Top Gun* of Tom Cruise buzzing the tower would mentally put me right back into that Phantom.

Seeing the carrier from the air, the thought of trying to land looked like aiming for a postage stamp. You're barreling toward this tiny target at 150 mph and then—bam!—you're jerked to a stop in three seconds. Somehow, I managed to keep my lunch down, but you can bet I didn't jump at any more flight invites after that.

Flying in a military jet is nothing like commercial flights. The plane is constantly shaking and vibrating; it's a real strain on the body. This whole experience, originally just a prank by the pilots, ended up being incredibly enlightening for me.

Aboard the ship, I was the guy staring at radar screens, tracking blips that represented planes. Flying with the pilots showed me just how tough their job was, deeply reinforcing a crucial leadership lesson: truly understanding the challenges those under your wing face is what enhances your leadership. It taught me never to take lightly the demands we place on others.

This is why leaders who've been in the trenches, or who've engaged directly with frontline tasks, often end up more successful. They understand the true effort required to meet the demands they set. Just as some of history's greatest military leaders led from the front, experiencing firsthand what it was to be under fire, successful business leaders immerse themselves in the daily operations of their companies.

In the business world, while we might not face life-and-death situations, the principle of direct involvement remains vital. If you run a supermarket, spend an hour bagging groceries. If you own a restaurant, take a shift bussing tables and washing dishes. If you manage a trucking company, take a turn behind the wheel. It's challenging to effectively lead and say "just do it" without understanding the particulars of the tasks involved.

Understanding the practical side of operations is not just beneficial, it's crucial. Many business failures stem from leaders who don't fully grasp what they're asking their teams to accomplish. Having immersed yourself in the tasks you oversee is as critical as any strategy taught in business school.

WELCOME PROBLEMS: WORRY ABOUT WHAT YOU DON'T KNOW

The Avengers and friends are preparing for their final showdown with Thanos, the ultimate bad guy of the universe, in *Avengers: Infinity War*, when Dr. Strange performs a bit of intelligence gathering. He uses his powers to look into the future, scanning through all the possible outcomes of the battle ahead.

When his teammates ask how many futures he saw, Dr. Strange replies, "Fourteen million, six hundred and five."

And when Iron Man presses him, *How many of those include us winning?* Dr. Strange gives a chilling one-word answer:

"...One."

Dr. Strange can travel through time to understand what's coming.

As a CEO, you can't. That's why you have to find your own way to gather intelligence—because the unknowns are your biggest threat.

I knew a billionaire who understood that better than anyone.

Every now and then, sometimes first thing in the morning, sometimes in the middle of a busy workday, you'd hear him before you saw him. He'd be walking through the halls of his company, booming voice echoing off the glass and drywall:

"BRING ME THE PROBLEMS!"

Not solutions. Not status reports. Problems.

He didn't whisper it in boardrooms or bury it in memos. He *shouted* it, like a preacher calling for repentance or a coach firing up a team. And it wasn't just a slogan. It was a mandate.

I watched people test him at first. They'd bring small things, errors in supply chain, questionable marketing copy, unhappy clients. And he'd listen. Never once did I see him fault someone for showing up with a problem.

But if someone knew about an issue and didn't bring it forward? If he found out that a fire had been smoldering somewhere while folks pretended all was well? That's when the mask came off. That's when you saw the other side of "BRING ME THE PROBLEMS." The guy was ruthless with people who hid things, especially if they hid them to protect their egos, or worse, to protect *his*.

He used to say, "A problem hidden is a problem multiplied." And that stuck with me. Still does.

I've come to think of a business the way you'd think of a person with early-stage cancer.

Let's say this person has a physical scheduled with their doctor. If they show up, if they're honest, if they talk openly about the weird pain they've been feeling, the fatigue, the small but nagging changes, then the doctor has a shot at catching something. They can run some tests. They can *find* the cancer, treat it, and maybe the person moves on with their life.

But what if they skip the checkup? Downplay the symptoms? Lie to the doctor—or worse, to themselves?

The cancer grows. Silently. Steadily. Until one day, it's too late to treat.

That's exactly what can happen to a company. And it's exactly why that billionaire walked the halls shouting for people to bring him the problems, he knew that silence was a killer.

He's not alone in that thinking.

One of the most legendary CEOs of Silicon Valley built an empire on that exact principle. Andy Grove, the former CEO of

Intel, wasn't just a brilliant engineer, he was a relentless problem solver, and even more importantly, a *problem welcomer.*

He captured it perfectly in the title of his bestselling business book:

Only the Paranoid Survive.

That wasn't just a catchy line. It was Grove's entire leadership mindset in five words.

Grove *wanted* to hear about threats, inefficiencies, disruptions because he believed that the greatest danger to a company wasn't competition, but complacency.

He created a culture at Intel where people were not just allowed, but *expected,* to speak up, challenge assumptions, and bring forward potential crises before they exploded. And he walked that talk.

In 1994, Intel's Pentium chip had a flaw, an obscure mathematical bug that only affected certain calculations.

At first, Intel's engineers knew about it but didn't think it was serious enough to be a public concern. Grove initially agreed, until he started getting letters. Then angry calls. Then media attention.

Instead of dismissing it, Grove took the hit *head-on.* Intel replaced thousands of chips, costing the company $475 million. He didn't try to spin it. He *solved it.*

He later said, "Bad companies are destroyed by crisis. Good companies survive them. Great companies are improved by them."

And Intel? It came out stronger.

Grove's style wasn't warm and fuzzy. He could be tough. But he *rewarded honesty* and challenged everyone, including himself, to look problems in the eye.

He even coined a phrase for it: "constructive confrontation."

At Intel, that meant anyone, regardless of title, was empowered to disagree with their boss if they believed something was off. His philosophy was simple and powerful: *silence equals danger.*

Sound familiar?

That's "Bring Me the Problems" in its rawest, realest form.

And the truth is, Grove was focused on something every leader should fear more than failure itself: unreported failure. The problems you don't know about. The ones festering in silence. The kind you learn about from pissed off customers that swear off doing business with you forever, and worse yet, tell everyone they know about it.

Because here's the human aspect, we all tend to hide things. Sometimes out of fear. Sometimes because we think, *It's not that bad*. Or, and this is more common than most leaders realize, we assume the person in charge already knows, and is either working on it . . . or ignoring it.

So we stay quiet.

No news, we figure, *is good news*.

And sadly, a lot of executives prefer it that way. It's easier on the ego to be seen as all-knowing. That illusion of control, of omniscience, it's seductive. It's often more gratifying, in the short term, to maintain the facade than to admit, *I didn't know that*.

But if you want to know whether a business is built to last, here's the test: look at the top. If leadership isn't actively creating space for honesty, and rewarding it, the foundation is already cracked.

Me? I prefer a culture where problems are not just accepted, but *expected*. Part of the cost of doing business. We're not here to pretend things go perfectly, we're here to fix what doesn't.

What's not acceptable is ignoring problems.

What's not acceptable is knowing something is wrong and staying silent.

What's *also* not acceptable is needing help and being too afraid, or too proud, to ask for it.

The only way to create this kind of culture is to *build it on purpose*. You have to encourage the organization, every layer of it, to bring conflicts, crises, and issues to the surface.

As a leader, that's your job.

You can't just sit behind closed doors and wait for honesty to knock. You have to go looking for it. That means walking the halls. Having casual conversations. Listening, without judgment.

It also means creating intentional, formal moments: company-wide meetings, open Q&As, anonymous feedback tools if that's what it takes. You say, *I want to hear what's going wrong.* Then—you prove it.

Because here's the truth: no amount of slogans or mission statements will build trust unless your *actions* reinforce them.

Culture isn't a poster on the wall. Culture is what you tolerate. Culture is what you reward.

So, every time someone steps up and says, *Here's a problem,* and you thank them, publicly, sincerely, you're setting the tone. You're showing everyone else that truth-telling isn't punished. It's prized.

And when you make a very public, very positive example of the people who embrace this mindset, something powerful starts to happen: You begin shaping the company around that mold. One act at a time. One conversation at a time.

In a turnaround, your people already know things have gone wrong. And they also know the leadership team that got them here probably didn't welcome the kind of feedback you're now asking for. They believe the nail that sticks out gets hammered down.

So show them you're different. Prove it.

You want a resilient organization? One that can adapt, survive, and grow?

Then walk the halls and shout it with me: "BRING ME THE PROBLEMS!"

ESSENTIAL #22

NEVER PANIC, AT LEAST NOT IN FRONT OF OTHERS!

In 2012's *The Avengers*, our heroes faced impossible odds during the Battle of New York. As waves of Loki's creatures flooded the city, Captain America didn't panic. He didn't even break a sweat. Instead, he calmly issued orders, telling Hawkeye to "take the rooftops, keep an eye out," and the Hulk to simply "Smash."

You either stay cool like Captain America, or you panic, and watch your mission fall apart before it even begins. I was one month into a new turnaround at Bristol Myers Squibb. Everything felt unfamiliar, new faces, new challenges, new expectations.

I was preparing for an all-employee meeting where I'd be handing out service awards to employees who had dedicated years, some decades, to this company. It was a great chance to introduce myself not just as the "new guy" at the top, but as the person who believed in where we were headed. I was going to deliver a message that was hopeful, optimistic, and energizing.

This was going to be a moment.

The room was already filling up. You could feel the buzz, people laughing, catching up, waiting to hear what this new leader had to say.

And then, about fifteen minutes before I was set to go on, the vice president of sales pulled me aside.

"We have a problem with Walmart," he said.

At that time, Walmart accounted for a full 20 percent of our company's revenue. So yes, my ears perked up. But I stayed calm. I nodded, took a breath, and said, "Okay. What's the problem?"

I was confident. New leader, big job, big stakes, this is what I signed up for.

"Walmart is very unhappy with the quality of our products and our packaging," he said.

Not insurmountable, I thought to myself. We can improve quality. We can redesign packaging. That's fixable.

"They're threatening to throw us out," he added.

That's . . . a much bigger problem, I thought.

"We also don't deliver on time to support their advertised promotions."

Holy crap, I thought. "Is that all?" I asked, half-joking but mostly hoping that was the end of the list. "No," he said, shaking his head. "Our pricing is too high. And there are new knock-off products from the competition that they'd rather go with."

Oh hell, I'm going to lose 20 percent of my sales a month after walking through the door.

Now, let's pause for a moment. That kind of news is the stuff that makes your stomach drop straight to the floor. You hear those words, and suddenly the whole weight of the business, its history, its people, its future, starts pressing down on your chest.

But here's the thing: I had a room full of people waiting on me. Waiting for a celebration. Waiting for their moment to be recognized. They weren't responsible for the Walmart disaster, and they sure didn't deserve a grim-faced, checked-out CEO who looked like he was five seconds from collapse. This wasn't about me.

You may not think you've signed up for a career in show business, but as a new leader, you are in the spotlight—and all eyes are on how you show up, communicate, and carry yourself. If I went into that room and didn't act the part of a confident leader, I would crush any hopes of fixing the organization.

So, I made a decision right then: I had to suck it up, for lack of a better phrase. I had to walk out there and do what leaders are supposed to do: show up, stay present, and lead. Because when you're speaking to a group, especially during a crisis, it's not just your words that matter. It's your energy. Your presence. Your body language.

You can say all the right things, but if your face shows panic and your shoulders slump with defeat, people will read you like a billboard. Humans are wired to pick up on body language. The disconnect registers instantly, and when it does, your message is lost.

All they remember is the worry you wore on your face.

Science backs this up. Studies show that when leaders speak, people respond more to how they say something than what they say. In fact, Dr. Albert Mehrabian, a psychologist and professor emeritus at UCLA, known for his groundbreaking work on nonverbal behavior, developed his classic "7–38–55" model reveals that:

- **7 percent** of perceived emotional meaning comes from the words themselves
- **38 percent** comes from tone of voice
- **55 percent** comes from facial expression, posture, and body language

So yes, when leaders communicate, their presence, tone, and physical cues often matter more than the actual content of their message.

In emotionally charged moments, like a crisis or high-stakes address, people are watching more than they're listening. And if there's a disconnect between your words and your body language, they'll believe what they see every time.

Another study, led by researchers at Princeton and NYU, found that people can size up a leader's confidence and credibility in a single glance. This phenomenon is called thin-slicing, our brain's ability to make quick, accurate judgments based on brief moments of visual information.

People don't just listen, they scan. And when you're standing in front of a room, they're thin-slicing you the whole time. Confidence is contagious. But so is panic.

Research in organizational psychology, particularly by Sigal Barsade and Olivia (Mandy) O'Neill at the Wharton School, shows that a leader's emotional state spreads rapidly through teams and organizations. It's known as emotional contagion, and it's especially powerful during moments of uncertainty or crisis.

Your anxiety, fear, or confidence doesn't stay contained; it ripples through your team faster than any memo. If your face says *We're doomed,* your team will believe it, even if your words are saying, *We've got this.*

So, when I say that people will forget your words and remember your worry, I'm not just being poetic. I'm being accurate.

The good news? You can learn to manage how you show up.

Here are several proven, practical techniques to help you suppress panic, manage nerves, and project calm when you're leading during a crisis. The key isn't pretending you're unaffected—it's learning how to control what you project and reset your nervous system in real-time.

1. Breathe Like a Leader
   Deep, diaphragmatic breathing activates the parasympathetic nervous system, which calms you down almost immediately. Navy SEALs rely on a technique called box breathing to stay grounded under extreme pressure. Before stepping into the room:
   • Inhale for 4 seconds
   • Hold for 4 seconds
   • Exhale for 4 seconds
   • Hold for 4 seconds

Repeat for 3–5 cycles. It grounds you, slows your heart rate, and helps keep your voice steady.

2. Plant Your Feet—Literally
   Leaders who pace, shift, or fidget send unspoken signals of anxiety, even if they're saying all the right things.
   Instead, stand tall with your feet shoulder-width apart. This simple stance sends a subconscious message of grounded authority, to your team and to your own nervous system.
   Keep your hands relaxed at your sides, or use them purposefully to emphasize key points. Stillness equals strength.

3. Slow . . . Down . . . Your Pace
   When nerves kick in, people tend to talk fast. But confident leaders know how to pause and own the silence.
   • Don't rush.
   • After making a key point, pause—breathe—let the room absorb it.
   • It helps you sound more in control and gives you a moment to reset your nerves.

4. Soften Your Face
   Before entering the room, take a moment to relax your face—especially your jaw, eyebrows, and eyes. Smile slightly (not fake—just enough to ease tension).
   This not only helps you project calm—it actually makes you feel calmer, thanks to a little brain trick called mirror neurons. People will reflect the calm they see in you.

5. Repeat a Grounding Mantra or Phrase
   Cognitive behavioral psychology shows that repeating a simple phrase can disrupt spiraling thoughts and center your focus. Performance coaches often suggest having a go-to grounding mantra, something you repeat silently to reset before speaking.

Try:
- "I'm steady."
- "They need me calm."
- "I've handled worse."
- "One step at a time."

Pick the one that fits you—and use it. Quietly. Just before you walk in.

6. Visualize the Calm, Not the Chaos
   Athletes, surgeons, and trial attorneys use this trick all the time.
   Picture yourself not just avoiding panic, but stepping in with clarity, walking into the room, connecting with people, projecting calm confidence. Visualization primes your brain to act as if it's already happened.

7. Lead with Questions or Acknowledgment
   You don't need all the answers to lead. You just need to show you're not paralyzed.
   Start with something simple and steady:
   - "I know this moment feels uncertain, but here's what I do know…"
   - "Let's take this one step at a time."
   - "We've been hit harder than expected—but we're still here, and that means we have a path forward."

I've always believed something that's proven true again and again: people trust steady hands more than perfect plans. And that's exactly what I tried to be.

So I walked out there. I stood tall. I smiled, not because everything was fine, but because I believed we could fix it. I gave a speech that acknowledged we had work to do, but reminded all that we had the grit and talent to get it done. I didn't lie. I didn't fake it. But I also didn't unload a crisis on people who had come to be honored.

There would've been no value, *zero*, in letting my panic steal that moment from them.

Yes, we lost the Walmart business. That's true.

But six months later? We got it back.

We fixed our quality. We improved our packaging. We tightened our delivery timelines. We got competitive on pricing. We earned our way back in, and we came out stronger. Our business was bigger and better than ever.

Looking back, I wouldn't change a thing about how I handled that day. Because if I had cracked, if I had let the weight of that conversation show through, what message would that have sent to the people in that room? That their celebration didn't matter? That our situation was hopeless? That the new leader folds under pressure?

People don't expect you to have all the answers. They just want a leader who believes the answers are *out there*, and believes in the people who can help find them.

As the old ad says: Never let them see you sweat.

ESSENTIAL #23

NEVER LET EGO OVERWHELM GOOD SENSE

Many superheroes have outsize egos to match their superhuman powers. Iron Man's oversized ego is famously brought to life by Robert Downey Jr.; can you even imagine anyone else playing Tony Stark? But for my money, the biggest ego in the Marvel universe belongs to Deadpool, the lovable rascal who straddles the line between hero and antihero.

Deadpool is completely full of himself. He slings rapid-fire jokes with the same ease that Spider-Man slings webs, and he rarely does anything that doesn't serve his own interests first. But in *Deadpool 2*, something shifts; he sacrifices himself to protect a teenager on the brink of becoming a villain. For once, it's not about him.

In business, I've seen a lot of leaders operate like early Deadpool: brilliant, fearless, and completely self-interested. That can get results, but it rarely builds loyalty. Teams follow vision, not ego. And in a turnaround, when morale is low and trust is fragile, people are watching closely: Are you here to save the company, or just make yourself look good?

Ego isn't the enemy. But if you don't learn to manage it, like Deadpool eventually does, it'll get in the way of everything you're trying to build.

I've seen that play out over and over. Confidence is essential, especially in high-stakes environments, but when it tips into arrogance, it clouds your judgment. That line between belief and blind spot is easy to miss, and even easier to cross.

The truth is that ego isn't inherently bad. It's like a power tool: extremely useful when handled with care, but dangerous if you're reckless. I've seen ego fuel bold decisions, decisive leadership, and real momentum. But I've also seen it unravel teams and tank potential.

You don't have to look far to see both sides of that reality play out in the real world.

Look at Adam Neumann, the co-founder of WeWork. Early on, his bold vision and charisma fueled explosive growth. But over time, his ego took center stage. The private jets, the billion-dollar valuation, the messianic talk about "elevating the world's consciousness;" it stopped being about the company and started being about him. When the IPO fell apart, so did the illusion. It was a classic case of ego overshadowing leadership. The business had promise. But what it needed wasn't a cult of personality; it needed trust, strategy, and execution.

The same dynamic played out at Uber under Travis Kalanick. He built a revolutionary company and was fearless in disrupting the status quo. But that same bravado created a toxic culture—one that prioritized aggression over accountability. Regulators were enemies, rules were optional, and inside the company, harassment and ethical blind spots were ignored. Eventually, the board had to intervene and Kalanick was forced out. His ego helped launch a global empire, but it nearly took it down too.

Contrast that with Satya Nadella at Microsoft. When he became CEO, the company wasn't in crisis—but it was stagnant. Rather than come in with a sweeping mandate or try to prove he was the smartest guy in the room, Nadella led with humility. He didn't ditch his confidence; he just kept it in check. He encouraged listening, collaboration, and self-reflection. And under his leadership, Microsoft transformed its culture, rebuilt trust internally, and reemerged as one of the most valuable companies in the world.

Neumann and Kalanick show what happens when ego goes unchecked. Nadella shows what's possible when it's harnessed with purpose.

That contrast isn't just theoretical. I've lived it. In my four decades serving on both for-profit and nonprofit boards, ranging from startups to public companies, I've watched my own ego come into play more than once. I like to think it's been a force for good. But only when kept in check.

I still remember my first board seat, Waterpik, a then-public company best known for its dental hygiene products. That role opened the door to a long journey across boardrooms, where I'd take on roles as chairman, CEO, and head of everything from audit to compensation committees. Each position brought its own challenges, and plenty of chances to test whether my ego was working for me or against me.

My background in navigating the complexities of public companies equipped me with a unique set of skills and knowledge, a reservoir I often drew upon in board meetings dominated by relatively inexperienced members who were there for their marquee value.

It wasn't about being the smartest in the room; it was about being the most knowledgeable in specific areas critical to our governance and compliance, especially those related to the intricate regulations of the Securities and Exchange Commission (SEC).

In these boardrooms, the balance of ego was crucial. Recognizing my own expertise didn't stem from a place of arrogance but from a genuine understanding of my own capabilities and experiences relative to others in the room.

During discussions on compliance and SEC reporting, areas fraught with pitfalls, my role often shifted from director to educator. In those moments, ego wasn't a shield to assert dominance; it became a beacon, allowing me to lead colleagues through the fog of regulatory complexity.

In delicate situations where the board could easily guide a company into trouble with regulators, my ego was my ally. It empowered me to assertively step forward, to educate and lead discussions on critical issues where misunderstanding the rules could lead to significant consequences for the company. My ego, tempered with a sense of duty and a commitment to good governance, helped steer our company through potential crises by fostering a culture of compliance and informed decision-making.

Reflecting on these experiences, it's clear that while ego can indeed overwhelm good sense if left unchecked, it can also play a crucial role in leadership. The key is to harness it, to let it fuel your confidence without letting it cloud your judgment. When you find that balance, ego transforms from a personal trait into a tool for collective success.

Ego, when managed well, isn't just about asserting one's importance; it's about recognizing when your unique contributions can lead, guide, and educate others. It's about knowing when to step up, and equally, when to step back, allowing your experiences to speak and act when they matter most.

So, in these boardrooms, my experiences have not only been about managing the complexities of corporate governance but also about navigating the interpersonal dynamics that can influence a company's direction. The presence of ego? Yes, it exists, but more often than not, it manifests in its positive form, driving decisions backed by expertise rather than mere self-interest.

Let's go back to that question, what *is* the difference between ego and confidence?

All human beings have an ego. It's not about whether you have one, it's about how your personality expresses it. Some people carry their ego quietly. Others . . . not so much.

And sometimes, what looks like a big ego is actually masking the opposite. In my experience, people with low self-esteem, who don't feel important or validated, can often come off as overly aggressive or controlling. It's not that they're confident. It's that they're trying to convince *themselves* that they're worthy by trying to dominate the room or impress everyone in it. I've seen it plenty of times. You probably have too.

The worst cases, though, are the ones who are genuinely convinced they're God's gift to the rest of us. That kind of unchecked ego can derail teams, projects, even companies. And while you hope to avoid people like that, the reality is you're going to run into them at some point in your career.

That leads naturally to a moment of reflection, one that touches on something I've come to value over the years: recognizing the times when ego, in hindsight, may have gotten in the way of making the best decision for my team or, in this case, my family.

Because some of the best leadership lessons don't come from the office. They come from home.

We've talked about this as a family, and I have no problem saying it publicly: my wife deserves 90 percent of the credit for how great our sons turned out. I mean that sincerely. She was the one at home raising them, being present, engaged, patient, while I was off being Mr. Businessman. I was running around the world, running companies, running deals, and more often than not, running on empty.

And then I'd come home.

After a week away, sometimes more, I'd walk through that front door like I was still in the corner office. As if I were the king of the family again. Instantly. No warm-up. No check-in. Just . . . I'm back, let's do things my way.

And it didn't go over well.

It didn't take long to realize my family had been doing just fine without me. In fact, they were thriving. They didn't need a CEO walking through the door, disrupting the rhythm they had built— they needed a husband and father willing to join, not command.

That wasn't easy to accept, and it happened more than once. But eventually, I had to admit they were right.

That realization hit harder than any boardroom confrontation. It forced me to ask why I felt the need to reassert control the moment I came home. The answer was ego, not the loud, attention-seeking kind, but the subtler version that whispers, *things couldn't have run well without me.*

And I was wrong.

Those moments taught me a lesson I carried back into my professional life: leadership isn't about asserting presence; it's about earning it. It means recognizing when systems are working just fine and asking, *Where can I add value without getting in the way?*

I started to think more deliberately about the dynamic in every room I walked into. Whether it was a board meeting or a leadership off-site, I'd ask myself: *Am I stepping in because I have something meaningful to contribute? Or because my ego needs to be heard?*

That shift in thinking changed the way I led teams. I found myself listening more, especially in the early stages of a turnaround or transition. I'd still speak up when necessary, when my experience could help navigate risk, clarify direction, or educate, but I became more intentional about *when* and *how* I did so.

I realized that confidence is quiet. It doesn't demand attention. It doesn't need to bulldoze the room. Confidence allows space for others to speak. Ego, unchecked, often tries to fill that space before it's even open.

That distinction has served me well ever since. And it came not from a corporate crisis or legal battle, but from coming home and realizing my sons didn't need a leader. They needed a father, a listener.

Ego is part of who we are. It can drive ambition, sharpen instincts, and give us the courage to speak up. But it has to be managed, tempered with self-awareness and grounded in purpose.

I've learned, often the hard way, that real leadership isn't about who talks the most or commands the spotlight. It's about knowing when to lean in and when to get out of the way. Influence isn't measured by volume; it's measured by value.

So no, I don't try to silence my ego. I just ask it to sit next to good sense. Because when those two work in tandem, that's when the real magic happens.

And if you ever forget the difference? Come home after a week away and try to take over dinner. That'll remind you real fast.

All of which is to say—ego isn't the enemy, unless you let it be.

Even Deadpool figured that out.

MAINTAIN YOUR ENERGY, MENTAL AND PHYSICAL

I'll tell you something that doesn't get said nearly enough in leadership circles, especially in turnarounds, where the pace is brutal and the stakes are high: a macho attitude will break you.

That relentless "no rest, no weakness, no distractions" mindset might look tough from the outside. It gets applause in movies. But in real life? It's a fast lane to bad decisions, burnout, and broken teams. And in a turnaround, bad decisions are luxuries you can't afford.

You have to protect your most valuable asset: your judgment. And judgment only works when your mind and body are fully functional. That means rest. That means exercise. That means, not kidding, eating something green once in a while. I learned this the hard way, like most important things in my career as a turnaround expert.

Let me tell you exactly how.

I was working with a guy, he was around fifty, who was doing a great job on some projects for our family business. Incredibly hardworking. Incredibly kind.

He also had a heart condition. One day, he quietly showed me the scar down the middle of his chest. He wasn't even allowed to drive. But unless he told you, you'd never know. He just kept show-ing up. No complaints. No drama. Just total dedication.

One weekend, I got a call from his wife. He'd passed away, at his desk.

I didn't press for details. I assumed it was his heart. I was shocked, saddened. And it stayed with me.

At the time, I was working in New York. I started noticing some-thing, every time I climbed out of the subway, especially after the third staircase, I'd be out of breath. Really out of breath. I figured I was just out of shape. Too many hours. Not enough workouts. Nothing serious.

But after my friend passed, I thought, *Maybe I should get checked out. It's been ten years since my last stress test. I'm sure I'm fine—but still.*

I was on the treadmill for maybe a minute before the cardi-ologist stopped the test, looked me in the eye, and said, "See me tomorrow."

Next thing I know, I'm in the hospital for an angioplasty. They sent a probe through my wrist and up into my heart.

The doctor said, "You've got two problems. First, what we call the widowmaker, that artery is completely blocked. The second one's partially blocked."

They placed two stents. The good news? I'd caught it early. No heart damage.

A few years later, I was in Santa Barbara on a business trip and got hit with a severe case of food poisoning. I was really sick. At one point, I felt a sharp pain in my chest. Thought I pulled some-thing. But after an hour, it still hadn't gone away.

Back to the hospital. Another angioplasty. Turns out the scar tis-sue from the original widowmaker stent had started to block the artery again. They placed a new stent inside the old one. I was out the next day. Another bullet dodged.

So finally, I asked my cardiologist, "How? I've never smoked. Never done drugs. My family lives into their eighties and nineties. How did this happen?"

He said, "Peter, now that I know you? The answer's simple. Stress."

He explained there are two kinds of people: those who feel stress, burnout, anxiety, the whole package, and those who carry it quietly. Internally. People like me. People who manage turn-arounds, navigate crisis after crisis, who stay calm and keep going. We don't feel much stress consciously. But it's there. Working on us. Quietly. Relentlessly.

That hit me hard. I thought I was doing everything right, but I wasn't taking care of the one system I needed most: me.

That's the real lesson.

In a turnaround, it's not just the company under pressure, it's you. If you burn out or drop dead at your desk, it doesn't matter how good your plan was. It ends there.

You might be killing it. But you still need insurance. Not paper-work—*real* insurance. Rest. Exercise. Family. Perspective.

Because leadership isn't just about pushing through. It's about lasting long enough to finish what you started.

And to do that, you need recovery time, not just physically, but mentally. You need space to reset your perspective before the next wave hits.

You also need escape time, and I don't mean weekends in Bermuda or mountain meditation retreats. I mean small, inten-tional moments where your brain can fully detach from the chaos.

For me, that kind of mental reset isn't optional, it's essential. It's how I stay grounded.

You could call it meditation, but not the cross-legged-on-a-yoga-mat kind. Mine looks a little different. Sometimes it's a quiet walk. Sometimes it's prayer, a favorite sport, or getting lost in a good detective novel. Other times, it's diving into stories of American history, Churchill, Gandhi, and many US presidents, not to study them, but to be inspired by them.

The common thread? I'm not the one making the next hard decision. That's the whole point. After a day full of real-world pressure and high-stakes calls, there's something deeply restorative about stepping into someone else's story for a while.

Honestly, those books are my mental naps. They give me the reset I need.

And hey—there's no shame in taking an actual nap, either.

It's a reminder that stepping away isn't an indulgence or a sign of checking out; it's a leadership tool that recharges your ability to think clearly, create boldly, and make the big calls when they matter most.

This isn't just about personal preference, it's strategy. The most effective leaders in the world don't leave their physical and mental energy to chance. They protect it. They invest in it. And they know that without mental clarity, physical stamina, and emotional balance, their decision-making suffers.

Warren Buffett once said, "I insist on a lot of time being spent, almost every day, to just sit and think." He spends up to 80 percent of his day reading and reflecting, not chasing meetings or obsessing over inbox zero, that modern-day badge of honor where every email gets answered immediately. He knows the best ideas don't come in a rush. They come in the quiet. I'm on board with the idea of carving out time to think, but for me, it's closer to 20 percent of the day. Enough to reset and stay sharp, without falling behind on what actually needs doing.

When Bill Gates was CEO of Microsoft, he carved out two full weeks every six months, completely unplugged, to ask the big questions and think creatively. He's speculated that it's part of his being on the autism spectrum, that he needs that kind of reset to stay sharp. He's said many of his best ideas came not during meetings or rapid-fire decisions, but in those slow, intentional pauses.

It's a fascinating approach, but it's not something I see myself doing. I've never been wired to step away for that long. My thinking time tends to come in shorter, more frequent doses, integrated into the rhythm of the day, not separated from it.

Oprah Winfrey has said she starts her day with five minutes of silence—no phone, no meetings, no distractions. "I center myself before I let the world in," she says. For her, clarity starts with quiet. She also swears by long walks and journaling to maintain perspective.

Microsoft's current CEO Satya Nadella finds energy in empathy. He reads widely, including poetry, to keep his emotional perspective sharp. "Empathy is not a soft skill," he says. "It's the hardest, and most critical, skill we develop as leaders."

Jeff Bezos has always been vocal about his need for eight hours of sleep. "I think better, I have more energy, my mood is better," he says. He also protects his mornings, scheduling high-stakes decisions only when he's at his sharpest. I get about eight hours too, and I've found the same to be true, clearer thinking, steadier energy, better judgment. It's not just about rest; it's about being mentally equipped to lead.

I learned the value of rest in the navy, not through structure or philosophy, but through survival. You sleep when you can, because tomorrow might not offer the chance. The watch rotations made full nights impossible, and there were times, truly, when I had to sleep standing up. That's not an exaggeration. That's just how it was.

So, I trained my body to rest wherever and whenever it could. Even ten minutes. Even on concrete. That mindset still guides me today.

When I'm running a turnaround, rest becomes part of my rhythm. My assistant knows: twenty minutes in the middle of the day, door closed, no interruptions. That's not me being lazy; that's me being smart. That nap resets my focus. It ensures the person walking into my office afterward gets the best version of me, not the burned-out one.

But rest is only part of it. If you want to stay mentally sharp, you've got to stay physically strong. There's no way around it.

In business, it's easy to put on weight just by doing your job. Lunch meetings, dinner meetings, late nights, constant travel, it wears you down. And worse, it slows you down.

If you're not moving your body, if you're not carving out time to train, you'll feel it in your brain before your belt. Your energy dips. Your judgment blurs. Your edge dulls.

That's why I move. That's why I train. Not to look good in a mirror, but to stay sharp in the fire. Because a leadership isn't a job. It's a fight. And if you're stepping into that arena every day, the least you can do is give your mind and body what they need to keep swinging.

The good news? Some companies are finally starting to get it. More and more are offering on-site physical therapy, wellness programs, and discounted gym memberships, not just as perks, but as smart strategy. Providers like PerformaX Elite and PT Solutions bring therapy directly into the workplace to prevent injuries, speed up recovery, and improve performance.

Amazon, for example, offers its "Active & Fit Direct" program, giving employees access to hundreds of gyms for a flat monthly rate. NVIDIA partners with programs like Crunch Fitness and also provides virtual training options, letting employees choose what works best for them.

Because here's the truth: you can grind yourself into the ground trying to be the hero—or you can step back, reset, and come back stronger. The people counting on you don't need you to be invincible. They need you to be present. Clear-headed. Energized.

The macho stuff? Leave that for the movies.

You can't lead others if your own system is running on empty. You can't think clearly, decide wisely, or show up consistently if you're burned out or running on fumes. The best leaders I know don't treat rest, reflection, or movement as indulgences, they treat them as performance strategies. They know what restores them, and they don't leave it to chance. They schedule it. They protect it.

Because this is real life, not a movie, not a motivational poster. The stakes are high. The pace is relentless. And the people counting on you don't need you to be a superhero, they need you to be present, clear-headed, and capable.

Even Tony Stark, genius, billionaire, Avenger, knew that his Iron Man suit couldn't run without power. He took time to recharge, recalibrate, and rethink. The strongest leaders do the same. They know when to push, when to pause, and when to close the door and take the damn nap.

REMEMBER THE DETAILS OF YOUR FAILURES—FORGET YOUR SUCCESSES

There's something about mistakes that sticks with me.

I'm sure, like you, I've always had a strong desire not to repeat them. Everyone makes mistakes; no one escapes that.

But for me, mistakes aren't just missteps. They're signals. They're lessons in disguise. I've found, more often than not, that we grow far more from our failures than from our successes.

Sure, success is fun. It's a moment to enjoy, to breathe. But for me? That moment lasts maybe five minutes. Then my mind kicks back into gear, scanning for what I *missed*. I've always had this underlying concern about the problems I don't yet know about. Success is nice. But it rarely teaches as deeply.

That doesn't mean reflecting on failure is easy. In fact, it's often the hardest kind of thinking there is. It's uncomfortable. It forces you to look at your own blind spots, sometimes patterns of them.

But that's exactly why it must be done.

When you step back and really examine the patterns in your mistakes, that's when you start learning what you're good at, what you're not, and where the danger zones are. Everyone has flaws.

Some of them are unfixable. But even the unfixable ones can be worked on, improved, managed.

Take me, for example. My impatience can be a good thing in turnarounds. But as a result I've always struggled to be a good listener—and it's caused damage over the years. I talk more about that in essential 4. I've worked on it, tried to show more respect for other viewpoints, and I've gotten much better. But let's be honest—if listening were a sport, I wouldn't be on the starting team.

Maybe that's why I've always admired leaders, especially the great ones, who were completely comfortable talking about their mistakes. They didn't dodge it. They didn't pretend they were infallible. What they cared about most was not repeating them. Their internal scorecard wasn't based on how many wins they racked up, but on whether they were improving, more aware, more in control, more resilient.

We all know the stories, iconic entrepreneurs who hit wall after wall before finally breaking through. These people weren't broken. They didn't see their failures as fatal. They saw them as formative. As education.

Sara Blakely, founder of Spanx, failed the LSAT twice and spent seven years selling fax machines door-to-door. She credits her mindset around failure to her father, who used to ask her at the dinner table, "What did you fail at today?" She once said, "My dad encouraged me to fail. That's how I learned that failure isn't the outcome, failure is not trying."

Brian Chesky, co-founder of Airbnb, was rejected by more than twenty investors and had to get creative just to survive. He and his co-founders sold collectible novelty cereal boxes labeled "Obama O's" and "Cap'n McCain's" during the 2008 presidential election to fund their company. Chesky has said, "Every time we launched and no one came, it was a lesson. We learned how to listen better, how to build better. That was the real education."

Whitney Wolfe Herd, after her public departure from the dating app Tinder, could have quietly stepped out of tech altogether.

Instead, she launched Bumble, a platform designed to flip the dating script by putting women in control. "I really believe being rejected from something good just means you're being pointed toward something better," she said. Her experience didn't weaken her; it clarified her purpose. She took the company public and became the youngest woman to do so in history.

None of them saw failure as the end. They saw it as the beginning of something better. They saw it as the training ground for what came next. That mindset matters. It's not just humility, it's strategic.

Nowhere is this mindset more essential than in fast-moving, high-stakes environments. When you're leading any organization through uncertainty or rapid change, you don't have the luxury of slow, perfect decisions. You're making calls constantly. And some of them won't be right. Not *might* be, *will* be.

In that kind of environment, the most important thing is to catch the bad calls quickly and reverse them even faster. That requires putting your ego aside. There's no time to protect your pride when the health of the organization depends on your ability to adapt and course-correct.

It's not about being right all the time; it's about being responsive, open, and committed to what works. You're not just making decisions. You're listening. You're adjusting. You're demonstrating to your team, your board, your investors, and your frontline employees that you care more about getting it right than being right. Sometimes getting it right and being right are the same thing. How you react when they aren't will tell your team a lot about you as a leader.

There's absolutely nothing wrong with saying, "I was wrong." Or, "I changed my mind." In fact, when those changes are influenced by feedback from your team, it's one of the fastest ways to build trust. It shows that you're not just *hearing* people, you're *listening*.

Here's the last piece, and it's just as important: once you understand your failure, once you've unpacked the why, move on.

Sit with it. Own it. But don't live in it. Internalizing a lesson is one thing. Becoming consumed by it is another. At a certain point, dwelling becomes quicksand. It traps your energy, your creativity, and your forward motion.

Richard Branson, founder of the Virgin Group and a lifelong risk-taker, once said, "You don't learn to walk by following rules. You learn by doing, and by falling over." It's a reminder that failure isn't just acceptable, it's essential. You stumble, you adapt, and you grow stronger. What matters most is not avoiding mistakes, but having the courage to keep moving through them.

Most famously, Thomas Edison, whose work laid the foundation for modern invention, said, "I have not failed. I've just found 10,000 ways that won't work."

Failure hurts. Whether it's a quiet misstep or a high-profile crash, the emotional sting can be real, and lasting. But how we respond to that failure often matters more than the mistake itself.

Over time, psychologists, researchers, and coaches have identified a set of best practices that can help you not just recover from setbacks, but come back stronger because of them.

1. **Lead with Self-Compassion**
   One of the most powerful ways to move forward, and one of the most overlooked, is self-compassion. Kristin Neff, a professor at the University of Texas and one of the top voices on the subject, has found that treating yourself the way you'd treat a friend in the same situation can ease anxiety, quiet the inner critic, and actually help you stay motivated. So instead of saying, "I blew it," try, "That was tough—but I'm learning. I'll do better next time."

2. **Define the Mistake—Then Define the Lesson**
   Naming what went wrong is step one. But naming what you learned is what moves you forward. Taking a

few minutes to reflect (or even journal) on three simple questions can be transformative:

- What happened?
- What was in my control?
- What would I do differently next time?

Experts suggest this process activates your brain's learning centers and begins to counteract the emotional charge of failure.

3. **Zoom Out and Get Perspective**
When you're in the middle of a failure, it can feel like your whole story. But psychologists advise "zooming out" to see the big picture. That one botched deal, bad hire, or wrong call is just a chapter—not the whole book. Failure isn't an identity. It's a moment.

4. **Reframe the Narrative**
As self-development author and speaker Dr. Wayne Dyer once said, *If you change the way you look at things, the things you look at change.* That's the heart of this practice. Reframing is a cornerstone of cognitive-behavioral therapy (CBT); it's about shifting how *you* interpret what happened. Instead of thinking, *"I'm not cut out for this,"* try, *"That strategy didn't work—what else can I try?"* When you move from judgment to curiosity, you create space to learn, adapt, and grow stronger from the experience.

5. **Take a Small, Purposeful Step Forward**
Martin Seligman, one of the founders of positive psychology, found that action, no matter how small, is one of the most effective antidotes to helplessness. Call a mentor. Rework the plan. Try again. Movement creates momentum, and momentum creates confidence.

6. **Create, and Lead in a Growth-Oriented Environment**

   Whether you're leading yourself or a team, normalize failure as part of the process. The most resilient organizations don't just reward results, they value learning, iteration, and honesty. Leaders who own their own failures, without shame or spin, send a powerful message, Most mistakes are not career-ending. They're character-building.

7. **Don't Over-Identify With the Mistake**

   A key principle in modern psychology is this, you are not your worst moment.

   Say, "I made a mistake," not "I am a failure." That small shift in language reshapes how your brain stores the experience. It becomes something you lived through, not something you are.

   No Marvel hero better illustrates the weight of failure than Peter Parker. After gaining his powers, Peter makes a selfish choice, not stopping a robber when he easily could have. That decision leads directly to the death of his Uncle Ben, the person who loved and raised him. That failure defines him more than any victory ever could.

   Even after saving countless lives, Peter never forgets that moment. It becomes his compass. As he puts it, "When you can do the things that I can, but you don't, and then the bad things happen? They happen because of you."

   He doesn't lead with his wins; he leads with the lesson that changed everything. Moving on from failure isn't about pretending it didn't happen. It's about understanding it, owning it, and then refusing to let it define what comes next. Mistakes are inevitable. Growth is optional.

ESSENTIAL #26

DON'T EMBRACE THE "CULT OF THE CEO": DON'T WRITE A BOOK ABOUT YOUR ADVENTURES WHILE YOU'RE ON THE JOB

In the whirlwind of leading a high-impact initiative or major change effort, it's easy for you, as the CEO or any visible leader, to find yourself catapulted into the spotlight. Suddenly, you're not just a CEO; you're a celebrity. This spotlight can be intoxicating, but beware, it's also a trap that can distract from the real work at hand. There's a reason I waited until *after* my corporate career to write this book, and you're about to find out why.

After I took the reins as CEO of Marvel, I found myself featured in major business magazines, honored at the university where I studied, and appearing on financial news networks. These events were flattering but also a reminder of the new pressures and visibility that came with my role.

Over the last few decades, the media has glorified the title of "chief executive officer" to the extent that the fate of entire organizations, regardless of their size, is often depicted as resting solely on the shoulders of the CEO. Whether you're leading a startup, driving a major transformation, or navigating intense market pressure, you're often portrayed in extremes—either heralded as a heroic savior or derided as a complete failure. It's this black-and-white portrayal that feeds into the "Cult of the CEO," where personal brand overshadows corporate performance. The problem often begins when CEOs start believing their own press. The tales of CEOs who absorbed their own hype are numerous and cautionary. They start thinking they are infallible, appearing regularly on TV and weighing in on topics far removed from their expertise, often coming across as out of touch or superficial.

There are various opinions on the impact of CEOs becoming the "face" of their companies. Experts note that while a visible CEO can enhance a company's reputation and personify its corporate values, this strategy comes with risks and requires careful handling.

A CEO's visibility can humanize the brand, making it more relatable and trustworthy to consumers. When CEOs effectively communicate and embody the organization's values, they can enhance brand perception and drive business.

However, there are potential downsides. If a CEO becomes too prominent, they might overshadow the broader company goals or alienate stakeholders if their personal views or actions conflict with the company's values or public expectations. Overexposure can lead to a focus shift from company achievements to the CEO's personal characteristics or opinions, which might not always align with the company's interests.

The key to leveraging a CEO's visibility effectively lies in maintaining a balance—ensuring that their public persona and communications align closely with the company's strategic goals and values. It's important that CEOs use their visibility not just to elevate their own profile but to substantively engage with and advance the company's objectives.

The sense of invincibility often seen in CEOs who are constantly in the media spotlight, sets the stage for leaders like Steve Jobs, whose persona at Apple transcended even the brand itself, embodying its innovation and quality.

However, this prominence also brought challenges, particularly during his health issues and after his passing, raising concerns about Apple's future leadership. Jobs's overwhelming presence sometimes overshadowed other team members, affecting internal dynamics and succession planning. This was starkly illustrated by the chatter years after Jobs' death, in which tech industry watchers wondered when Apple would finally run out of ideas left behind by their visionary leader.

This critical reliance on Jobs's personal brand meant that any news about him could swing perceptions drastically, a situation not unlike when a high-profile business magazine trivially focused on an internet CEO's daily schedule, highlighting the thin line between personal branding and corporate substance. It not only cast the CEO in a poor light but also highlighted a disconnect from the real challenges of the business.

Similarly, many CEOs write books under the guise of offering leadership insights, but these often serve more to glorify their own image than to provide genuine guidance. I can hardly get past the first few pages; they're often ghostwritten and read like a self-tribute rather than anything genuinely insightful. It's pretty much an ego trip on paper, which must be just as confusing for their teams as it is annoying for readers.

Such distractions are not just minor annoyances. They can divert a CEO from essential tasks. Achieving success in a turnaround isn't just about weathering the storm; it's about navigating forward without losing sight of your origins or future goals. When accolades start rolling in, staying grounded is crucial. The essence of your role isn't to bask in the limelight but to fortify your company against future challenges.

Doug McMillon's journey from unloading trucks to becoming the CEO of Walmart exemplifies dedication and an understanding of every company level. Known for his down-to-earth demeanor, he prioritizes company culture, sustainability, and community impact over personal recognition. McMillon champions initiatives that bolster Walmart's societal role, advocating that good business practices and positive community actions go hand in hand. He has expressed this sentiment by noting, "Like people, when companies work to foster a culture of collaboration, communication becomes second nature."

Similarly, Tony Schwartz, CEO of The Energy Project, underscores the importance of humility in leadership. He openly shares his mistakes with his team, which helps in building trust and fostering a more relaxed work environment. This candid approach resonates with the notion that effective leadership is as much about personal integrity and vulnerability as it is about strategic decision-making.

In a like manner, Kevin Chou, the co-founder and former CEO of immersive multiplayer mobile game developer Kabam, has said how he had to revise his early belief that a CEO needed to "have all the answers." Instead, Chou emphasizes the importance of asking insightful questions, assembling a strong team, and maintaining an open mind in decision-making processes. He noted, "I learned that it was less about having all the answers and more about facilitating the team in a way that supports their success. This meant setting aside my ego and prioritizing service to my team above all."

Ultimately, the role of a CEO during a turnaround is complex and fraught with the temptation to become a celebrity. However, the most effective leaders resist this allure, opting instead for strategic leadership that prioritizes long-term success over short-term fame. By focusing on sustainable, substantive progress, they can avoid the pitfalls that have ensnared many others.

HAVE THE COURAGE TO ACT WHEN CHANGE IS MANDATORY FOR SURVIVAL AND SUCCESS

You don't need a boardroom full of analysts or a mountain of reports to tell you a company's in trouble. Most of the time, you can feel it the moment you walk through the door. There's a heaviness in the room, a kind of quiet desperation that's impossible to miss. And that's when I know: we're not talking about optional transformation here. This is survival mode.

It's like walking into a house where no one wants to admit it's on fire.

I've stepped into several companies on the brink of collapse. Not just declining, collapsing. And the truth is, when change is mandatory, it's not a quiet whisper. It's a siren.

Sometimes, the signs are right there in print: negative press, dwindling revenues, public filings that practically shout "mayday." If it's a public company, you can pull their numbers from the SEC website and see it all in black and white. If it's private, the first thing I ask for on day one is the financials. The trends never lie. They show you exactly how bad it is—and whether you're dealing with a slow bleed or full-on cardiac arrest.

I've never been invited in when things are going great. No one hires a guy like me just to kick the tires. They call because they're out of options. The former leadership is gone—or on the way out. And everyone inside knows it, even if they won't say it out loud.

So, when people ask me, "How do you recognize that change isn't just necessary, but mandatory?" I tell them: *the signs are everywhere. You just have to be willing to look.*

But here's the bigger question: *Why do so many wait until it's too late to act?* That's what really fascinates me. You can see the cliff coming. It's in the data, the culture, the headlines. But some leaders stay frozen, hoping the storm will pass, the market will shift, or that some miracle will arrive just in time.

It rarely does.

Waiting until you're forced to act is what gets companies killed. Courage means moving *before* you're cornered. Acting when the road ahead looks risky, uncertain, even terrifying. That's the kind of leadership it takes to turn a company or organization around. But most leaders don't make that move until they've run out of less painful options.

There's another thing you learn quickly in a turnaround: when "leaders" never should've been in leadership in the first place, it shows. Fast.

This is where things get tricky, not because the problems are hard to see, but because they're wrapped in ego, legacy, and sometimes misplaced loyalty. You've got founders or CEOs who were brilliant in the early stages. Builders. Visionaries. But they held on too long. They believed their instincts would always be right, even when the data, and the team, were screaming otherwise.

In any turnaround, you often find that the culture is paralyzed by fear, fear of change, fear of accountability, fear of conflict. Leading through this means you can't just tiptoe around. You need to walk in through the front door and start dismantling what doesn't work, not to destroy, but to rebuild something stronger, something that can actually endure.

The real courage comes not from having all the answers but from clarity, recognizing the truth, stating it boldly, and taking decisive action, especially when you expect resistance.

You either act, or the company fails. That's the stark reality.

One thing I've learned, and it's foundational, is that you can't fix a company without first addressing its culture. And if those at the top are unwilling to embrace change, any effort at a turnaround is doomed from the start.

Maybe in a company that's doing okay, you can be incremental, cautious, strategic. But in a company that might not exist a year from now? A place where hundreds of jobs are on the line? You swing big. You swing smart, but you swing hard. There's no other option.

There's no such thing as a "safe bet" when a company is circling the drain. If you're afraid to shake the tree, you're just waiting for it to fall over.

If you need proof of what happens when bold moves aren't made, look no further than Blockbuster, once the titan of the video rental industry. Despite its dominance, with thousands of stores across the nation, Blockbuster faced a pivotal challenge when a small mail-order DVD service named Netflix emerged, offering convenience, personalization, and no late fees. Underestimating this threat, Blockbuster even passed on the opportunity to purchase Netflix for just $50 million.

Stuck in their ways, focused on their brick-and-mortar model, Blockbuster ignored the shift toward digital streaming. By the time they attempted to launch their own digital service, it was too late. Netflix had already redefined the industry, leading to Blockbuster filing for bankruptcy in 2010.

Similarly, Toys "R" Us, once a dominant player in the retail toy industry, faced a steep decline by not adapting quickly enough. Saddled with significant debt from a leveraged buyout in 2005, the company struggled to invest in essential areas like e-commerce and store modernization.

As shopping trends increasingly shifted online, Toys "R" Us could not compete effectively with giants like Amazon, Walmart, and Target, who were rapidly enhancing their digital platforms and optimizing logistics.

This inability to keep pace with technological and market changes led to their bankruptcy in 2017 and the closure of all its US stores by 2018.

Additionally, while competitors enhanced both their digital platforms and in-store experiences, Toys "R" Us lagged behind. Its stores remained largely unchanged, missing the chance to become vibrant, experiential destinations. And online, it never caught up to retail giants like Amazon, Walmart, and Target, leading to the collapse of its more than sixty-year market presence.

Similarly, Borders faced its own challenges with adapting to the digital era. In a pivotal decision in 2001, instead of developing its own online bookstore, Borders outsourced its online sales to Amazon. This move not only drove customers to a competitor; it delayed Borders' own digital learning curve and left them playing catch-up for years. By the time Borders reclaimed its online sales operation in 2008, it was significantly behind its competitors. Unable to recover, Borders filed for bankruptcy in 2011.

These stories of Blockbuster, Toys "R" Us, and Borders illustrate the importance of innovation and adaptability in business survival. Each company observed changes in the market but failed to act swiftly or effectively enough to implement the necessary transformations. Their inability to evolve ultimately led to their downfalls, underscoring just how essential innovation and adaptability are to long-term survival.

So, what really kills companies? Complacency. It's the belief that what worked yesterday will continue to work tomorrow, that customers will wait for you to catch up, that innovation can take a back seat while you rest on your laurels. That mindset is exactly what I confronted in some turnarounds.

Nowhere is this more relevant than with today's biggest disruptor: AI. If you're not paying attention to how rapidly AI is reshaping industries, altering workflows, shifting customer expectations, and transforming entire business models, then you're asleep at the wheel. Most people recognize AI's significance; the real issue is that not everyone is proactive about integrating it into their operations.

This lack of proactivity is a cultural flaw. Too many companies treat evolution as just another item on their to-do list. They're not actively monitoring technological shifts, changes in consumer behavior, or even cultural mood swings that could dramatically affect their bottom line. They take stability for granted, which is not just outdated, it's dangerous.

I've always believed that staying on top of change isn't optional; it's a responsibility. The companies that survive, and thrive, are those that embed this proactive approach into their DNA. Because here's the truth: survival isn't about weathering the storm. It's about evolving your business while the storm is still on the horizon.

To ensure your company remains vibrant and viable in a rapidly changing marketplace, ask yourself daily: What am I doing today to prepare for tomorrow's challenges? Merely reacting isn't enough; you must anticipate changes. Foster a culture where innovation is routine, and resilience is built into everything you do.

In business, change is the only constant, and how you manage it will define your future success or failure. Being proactive could mean the difference between leading the market and becoming a cautionary tale.

KNOW WHEN IT IS TIME TO GO

In my career, I've usually spent about three years as CEO during corporate turnarounds. This timeframe suits companies not bogged down by heavy regulations, allowing us to implement substantial changes and rejuvenate a corporate culture.

Honestly, I'm hooked on turnarounds; it's like an addiction for me, maybe even a flaw. But I know that overstaying my welcome after the job is done can leave me feeling like Spider-Man without his web-shooters: still capable, sure, but missing what gets me excited and truly makes me effective.

This three-year cycle isn't random; it matches the complexity involved in transforming a business across various international markets, where each requires tailored strategies and cultural sensitivity.

For instance, while a US-based company might be turned around in just a year, international giants like Marvel or Remington often require up to three years. This extended timeframe isn't just about tackling domestic issues; it's also crucial for aligning and integrating operations across the varied global landscapes.

In contrast, my role as chairman at electroCore, a medical technology company, brought a unique set of challenges, mainly due to strict regulatory demands. I'll get into more details about the company later in the chapter, but it's important to mention that achieving a turnaround took five years. The delay was primarily caused by significant bureaucratic obstacles and the necessity for thorough scientific validation and clinical trials before we could launch new products.

This experience highlights how different industries require tailored strategies, especially when innovation depends on navigating regulatory frameworks and leveraging creative talent. Whether it's in filmmaking, comic book production, medical technology, or even consumer products like hairdryers, where creativity often surpasses technological hurdles, it's crucial to consider the specific metrics that will define the success of a turnaround.

When I think about how you really know meaningful progress has taken hold, it boils down to a few clear indicators. First, the financial health of the company—such as profitability and sales growth—is a straightforward measure and often the first sign that the efforts are paying off.

Another vital measure is Key Performance Indicators (KPIs) specific to the industry, like box office performance or market share in comic books. For example, at Marvel, when I started, we had the second best market share in the comic book market; by the time I left, we had the leading market share by a significant margin. These metrics are concrete evidence that the company isn't just surviving; it's leading.

But numbers only tell part of the story. The true testament to a successful turnaround lies in the company culture, the values system instilled. It's about ensuring that the changes will outlast my tenure. Have I managed to instill a culture that will thrive even after I'm gone?

That's my legacy. Observing daily interactions gives me a good sense of whether this new culture has taken root. This combination of financial health, KPIs, and cultural integration forms a comprehensive gauge of a turnaround's success, marking the point where I can step back, knowing I've achieved what I set out to do.

The essence of a turnaround CEO's role is to act swiftly, often relying on gut instinct and making bold moves rather than getting bogged down in prolonged deliberation. We are the mavericks who often sidestep conventional procedures to implement drastic changes, finding exhilaration in the face of daunting challenges.

Part of what makes this possible, and deeply fulfilling to me, is assembling and leading teams that can execute these rapid transformations effectively. I'm addicted to success through diverse teamwork. There's a profound sense of accomplishment in bringing together a group of talented individuals who can think on their feet, challenge each other, and rally around a common vision of turnaround success.

This team isn't just a group of employees; they're a cadre of problem-solvers who thrive under pressure, driven by the collective goal to pull the company back from the brink. Their resilience and ingenuity are crucial, making the seemingly impossible possible, and turning potential failure into a remarkable recovery.

Once the company is on solid footing with stable operations and the immediate crises, and the adrenaline rush of crisis management has subsided, I recognize the need to personally move on. In a calm environment, a turnaround CEO like myself can become disruptive without necessity, like a relief pitcher who struggles when his team is nine runs ahead.

You might think that after leading a successful turnaround, I'd be content to stay. However, I thrive on the turmoil and pressures of turning around a company, where each day brings new challenges, the norm is to challenge the status quo, cut through red tape, and make quick pivots.

However, when the dust settles and the company stabilizes, the leadership style required shifts dramatically. A stable company benefits from steady, consistent stewardship, leaders who can foster gradual growth and build strategies on broad consensus.

This is almost the antithesis of a turnaround CEO's modus operandi. Staying in a stable environment can lead to conflicts and might even undo the hard-won gains by overhauling systems that no longer need shaking up.

In my experience, this mismatch of leadership style with corporate needs often dilutes a company's core competencies, turning a successful turnaround into a gradual decline. At this point, I feel it's essential to step aside and get out of the way, allowing the company to continue thriving under new, more appropriate leadership.

About two and a half years into my tenure, I mentioned to the Marvel board that I was considering stepping down from active management. However, they asked me to stay on as CEO for another year. After that, I transitioned to the role of vice chairman of the board, where I focused primarily on investor relations for another six years.

I knew we were back on solid ground. It was clear that the company needed a new type of leadership to delve into areas like motion pictures, television, and interactive games, fields outside my wheelhouse. The company required executives who not only understood these industries but who were seasoned in managing the nuanced, steady growth that these sectors demand. I introduced you to some of those key executives back in essential #10.

Years later, I served as chairman of the board at electroCore, a medical technology leader advancing patient care. My role was advisory rather than hands-on, focused on guiding the company toward sustainable growth. It was a shift from my usual turnaround work, letting go, stepping back, and trusting the team to take things to the next level.

After five years as chairman, I announced my departure from the board a year in advance, capping off a rewarding journey. When I joined electroCore in 2020, the stock was priced at four dollars. Over the next four and a half years, we implemented a series of successful turnaround strategies. These efforts culminated in a dramatic increase in stock price, which jumped from $6 to $18 within just six months, reflecting the significant improvements we had achieved. The company became cash flow positive and completed a market-shaking acquisition, signaling its health and strategic vision.

This turnaround wasn't quick or easy. Unlike others I've led, this took nearly five years, largely due to the complexities of the medical technology industry. Navigating FDA regulations, compliance, and product claims takes time. But we succeeded, thanks in very large part to our CEO, Dan Goldberger. Dan made tough decisions, like cutting R&D costs while maintaining progress. He promoted talent, found efficiencies, and kept the board aligned—a true turnaround leader. I'd like to think that my past experience was a help to Dan because I understood what he was going through.

By the time I left, the company was stronger than ever, with a clear path forward. electroCore was thriving, and Dan is the right person to guide it into the future. As chairman, my role was complete. I had helped stabilize and rebuild the company, and now it was time to step aside, leaving it in capable hands.

The beauty of successfully leading a turnaround is that it opens doors to new opportunities. Proving your mettle in such a high-stakes role makes you a magnet for other companies needing revival. I quickly learned there is no shortage of mismanaged companies with the potential to transform into industry leaders.

But it's crucial to choose your next move wisely. I've made, and paid, for the mistake of not researching a company's culture before accepting the position. Instead, seek out another challenging, perhaps even perilous setting that demands your unique skills, where the thrill of transformation is alive.

In conclusion, knowing when to exit is as important as knowing how to lead the charge. It's about understanding not only your strengths and limitations but also what the organization needs to continue thriving without you.

For any leader, success isn't just about achieving results—it's also about knowing when to step aside, making room for new leadership that's aligned with where the organization is headed next. Letting go at the right time can be just as important as stepping up. This awareness is what separates good leaders from great ones—it's not just about the battles you win, but knowing when the war is over and it's time to pass the baton to others with the temperament for what is needed in the future.

FROM THE BRIDGE TO THE BOARDROOM

Looking back on this journey—from the bridge of a destroyer in Vietnam to the boardrooms of some of the world's most iconic companies—what strikes me most isn't just what I learned, but how I learned it.

I didn't set out to become a turnaround specialist. I simply wanted to lead well, solve meaningful problems, and bring out the best in people. And over time, I discovered that leading in crisis doesn't require superhuman strength, it requires something deeper: clarity, empathy, and relentless purpose.

What surprised me, again and again, was how often the real superpowers showed up in ordinary moments. A receptionist interpreting a smile, or the absence of one. A colleague brave enough to say, "You're not listening." A Comic-Con dad reminding me that corporate titles don't matter. These moments, often uncomfortable, became defining. They made me better.

The truth is, leadership is never about one person's brilliance. It's about the team. The mission. The culture you shape with every decision, every gesture, every act of listening. When people believe in where they're headed, and trust the person leading them, they'll do extraordinary things.

At Marvel, I saw firsthand what happens when a group of talented, determined individuals is given the freedom to dream big and the support to follow through. We didn't just turn a company around; we rewrote the rules of the industry.

But no turnaround, no transformation, is ever permanent. Every leader, every team, has to keep evolving. Keep listening. Keep learning. I've made my share of mistakes, and I've tried to own every one of them. That, too, is leadership.

If there's one message I hope you'll take from this book, it's this: You don't have to wear a cape to lead like a superhero. You just have to show up, every day, with courage, humility, and a commitment to do what's right, even when it's hard.

Leadership isn't about saving the day. It's about building a world where more people get to thrive. And that starts with you.

So take what's here. Make it your own. And remember, your greatest power as a leader isn't what you know or what you control.

It's how you make others feel about what they're capable of.

That's what changes companies. That's what changes lives.

That's what makes a superhero leader.

—Peter

ACKNOWLEDGMENTS

My great debt and admiration go to Joe Garner, the cowriter of this book and the author or coauthor of six *New York Times* best-sellers. Joe's guidance and knowledge for this project, and as the producer of our companion podcast, *Superhero Leadership*, were invaluable. The basis for this book actually started over ten years ago, thanks to my daughter-in-law, Eileen Cuneo. She used her writing skills to listen and record my initial thoughts on the twenty-eight essentials. These were a cornerstone for this book. My thanks also go to Jennifer Secor and Colin Cuneo, whose feedback was critical for this book and as associate producers for our podcast. Also, thanks to Michael Campbell of Skyhorse Publishing for his enthusiasm and support.

This book is really the product of the hundreds of individuals in my life who mentored and believed in me—those in my education, those in the US Navy, those in my personal and professional lives, and those in my family and my friends. Thank you all.

ABOUT THE AUTHOR

Forbes and *Business Insider* have called Peter Cuneo one of the best turnaround CEOs in America. Over four decades, he has led seven corporate transformations of both public and private companies, including Clairol, Black & Decker, Remington, and most notably, MARVEL Entertainment. Taking the helm in 1999, Peter rescued MARVEL from bankruptcy, guiding the company from a stock price of 96 cents per share to a $4.5 billion acquisition by Disney in 2009.

Peter's leadership foundation was forged in service. After graduating from Alfred University, he entered the US Navy, achieving the rank of lieutenant. He served as Damage Control Officer and Communications Officer aboard the USS *Joseph Strauss*, a guided missile destroyer that saw combat during the Vietnam War.

Following his naval service, Peter earned his MBA from Harvard Business School, where he received first-year academic honors and served as president of the International Business Club. He began his corporate career at W.R. Grace before spending fourteen years at Bristol-Myers Squibb, where he completed his first turnaround as president of Clairol's Personal Care Division. He went on to lead transformations at Black & Decker's Security Hardware Group and Remington Products before ultimately architecting Marvel's resurrection.

Today, as managing principal of Cuneo & Company, he partners with his sons to invest in and guide private companies in consumer, media, and entertainment sectors. He serves as chairman of OCSiAl, a nanotechnology company, and sits on the board of the National Archives Foundation. In 2016, he was awarded the Ellis Island Medal of Honor.

Beyond the boardroom, Peter is a sought-after speaker and passionate about using his experience to help educate the next generations of leaders. In 2024, he launched the *Superhero Leadership* podcast, exploring outstanding leadership through conversations with exceptional leaders across business, sports, and public service.

Most recently, Peter has extended his leadership teachings beyond the page and the mic. In 2025, he launched the Superhero Leadership App at Studio.com, offering users a personalized path to master the same principles that powered his success. The program provides a fully customizable experience that delivers practical, actionable guidance tailored to an individual's goals. Whether leading teams, reinventing a career, or sharpening decision-making, Peter hopes the app will help growing leaders become the hero of their own story—starting now.

Visit studio.com/petercuneo or scan the QR code to get the app.